Self-Employment

.... is it for you?

authorHOUSE®

AuthorHouse™ UK Ltd.
500 Avebury Boulevard
Central Milton Keynes, MK9 2BE
www.authorhouse.co.uk
Phone: 08001974150

First published by AuthorHouse 10/14/2011

ISBN: 978-1-4567-8894-0 (sc)
ISBN: 978-1-4567-8895-7 (e)

Self-Employment

...is it for you?

A Comprehensive Guide for Potential Entrepreneurs and Owners of Small and Medium Sized Businesses

by Walter A. Yates

Success or failure

Your checklist of what you should know before you start or your opportunity to improve the success of your business

Published by Author House

Typeset in Franklin Gothic by Park Graphics, Ormskirk, UK

BEFORE WE BEGIN

A list of tips that will fast-track a business to failure

1) Pursue the first idea that comes into your head

Imperative, once you've thought up a business idea or concept, don't waste a second and get it started without further ado. Why not start up a business you know absolutely nothing about, or even better look for those 'here today – gone tomorrow' business fads and ensure your new venture is gone tomorrow as well.

2) Avoid market research at all costs

Essential to guarantee failure, listen, nobody knows the market better than you, and what's a market anyway? You've spotted the opportunity and you'll only get rich quick if you get on with it and sell it to everybody you can. You'll just end up getting bored looking for a market niche with genuine needs and demands that you could meet.

3) Beat your competitors by selling at rock-bottom prices

Running a competitive business is just too easy. It doesn't matter how many competitors you've got, just make sure your prices are much lower than everyone else's. Don't worry about all that costing your product rubbish if you sell enough at ridiculously low prices you will be the customer champion in no time at all, which is the fast track to profit making. Isn't it?

4) Run a business that doesn't need any marketing

This is what it is all about. Your own brilliant ideas and keeping your friends impressed. Marketing is just a text book term anyway, isn't it? Why start broadcasting the reasons why your service is so good or offers such an affordable solution to a particular group of people, when all that will happen is that you end up giving your competitors a chance to copy all you ideas? Why would anyone want to give away their ideas? Start up a business that will promote itself, and where none of your competitors will have a clue what you're up to.

5) Don't worry about the cash

This is the best one. Everyone keeps telling you never to take your eye off your cash flow, but why bother with that when you've got the services of a good accountant and a sympathetic bank manager? They'll keep your finances straight, and let you know when there's no cash left. You just need to concentrate on being the overnight success you've always deserved to be.

6) Get advice from people who know nothing about running a business

There are plenty of 'experts' out there who'll gladly give you the benefit of advice that they may have read about or heard somewhere. Or even better, there are those serial business failures who'll give you even more tips like the ones we've given you here to make sure your new venture is a thoroughly spectacular flop.

It's a sad fact that some of you reading this will already be practising these tried and tested methods to guarantee the failure of your business.

Section One
THE PURPOSE AND GOALS OF YOUR BUSINESS

Contents
Section One

SECTION ONE

A – THE PURPOSE AND GOALS OF YOUR BUSINESS

A business has to have a purpose – this is not the same as describing the basic business concept.

A1 What is the purpose of the business – simply to provide sufficient income for you, or to grow into something else?

- To provide employment to/for:
- To be a business that...by
- To be the largest
  the only
  the most
  the best

A2 What are the goals of the business on the way to achieving its purpose? There may be several of them.

- To dominate the chosen market
- To secure a percentage of the chosen market
- To earn profits of....
- Customer satisfaction
- Customer loyalty
- To develop products to...

A3 How are you going to measure whether or not you achieve the goals? How are you going to measure success?

B – THE PRODUCT

There are two matters of almost equal importance – the product you are proposing to offer and the customers who will buy your product – and you cannot really separate the two – together they define the market you are in.

B1 **What are you offering?**

- Is it a service?
  Relying on your skill and experience? – How can it be developed?
- Is it a product?
  A material object?
  How can it be developed?
- Is it a combination of the two?
  How can it be developed?

B2 What are the key elements of your product?

- Is it a new idea, something not thought of before?
- Is it easy to copy?
- Can it be easily replaced by another product?
- Should it be patented?
- Is it a gimmick, a one off?
- Is it doing better something that is already available?
- Is it doing cheaper something that is already available

B3 What makes you product different from others on the market?

- What are its unique selling feature(s)?

B4 What are the benefits of the product to the customer?
HOW DO YOU KNOW?

B5 What are the strengths of the product? How are you going to build them?

B6 What are the weaknesses of the product?

- How are you going to eliminate them?

B7 Does your product meet the needs of the customer?
HOW DO YOU KNOW?

C – YOUR CUSTOMERS

C1 Who are your customers?

C2 Are these groups of customers?
- With different likelihoods of taking your product?
- Strong, good, fair and poor chance?

C3 What is the profile (description) of a typical customer or group?

C4 What are their requirements and needs?
- What is the most important think to them?

HOW DO YOU KNOW?

C5 How are you sure their needs are not already being satisfied?

C6 What influences your customers to buy or not to buy?

C7 What are the dissatisfaction factors of customers?

C8 How loyal are they likely to be to their current suppliers?

C9 How are the customer's needs and requirements going to change?

C10 What alternative sources of supply do your customers have (to you)?

IN SHORT

Why should a customer buy from you rather than your competitors?
Why should they part with their money to you?

D – THE MARKET PLACE

SIZE

D1 What has been the recent history of the market?

D2 Is the market static in size?
- Are you going to be fighting for market share or part of an increasing market?

D3 What affects the rate of change in market size?

D4 Are your customers all in one trade sector or is there demand in others?

D5 How are you going to make the market grow, or your share of it?

D6 What market research already exists in this field?

DEMAND

D7 Is demand
- For the product
  Increasing? Why?
  Decreasing? Why?
  Static? Why?
- In the area
  Increasing? Why?
  Decreasing? Why?
  Static? Why?

D8 What affects demand for the product? Consider:
- Economic Conditions
  Cyclical
  Are you entering at the right time?
- Employment/unemployment levels
- Environment
  Pollution
- Fashion and style
  Will the product become out of date quickly?
- Technical Development
  Will the product become out of date quickly?
- Weather
  Outdoor activities, food
  Seasonal Matters
- Competition
  Delivery, response time
  Price, Quality
  After sales service
- Location

- Status of customer
  Spending power
  Married/single/divorced/family
  Sex of customer, Car owner
  Home owner, Age
  Education, Qualification
  Social class, General lifestyle
  Health, Eating and drinking habits
  Exercise habits
- Status of general population –
  spending power
  Married/single/divorced
  Home owner, Age
  Education, Social class
  General lifestyle, Health
  Eating & drinking habits
  Exercise habits, Car owner
- How often the customer needs to buy the product – day of the week, time of the month, once a year?
- Is the product a need or a luxury?
- Is the product related to the demand for other product or services?
- Religion, ethnic and national origin
- Politics
- Convenience

D9 How will you cope with a falling demand?
- Change product?
- Move into a different line of business? – Reduce price?

D10 How will you cope with an increase in demand?
- Increase production?
- Increase price?

GEOGRAPHIC AREA OF BUSINESS

D11 How big is the market in terms of:
- Spending Power?
- Area?
- Number of customers?
- Number of suppliers?

D12 How quickly will the demand for your product build up?

D13 **What makes you believe there is room for another supplier in the market – you?**

PRICE

D14 What is the current range of prices?
- What causes the difference?

D15 What price will the market stand?
- How do customers view price?
  What is the product
  How do your competitors price
  worth to the customer?
  their product?
  Is price elastic?
- If you change the price a little will demand change a lot?
- If you change the price a lot will the demand stay much the same?
- How are you going to price your product?
  Will customers be suspicious of quality if it is too low?

HOW DO YOU KNOW?

SELLING

D17 How are you going to attract your customers?
- Advertising
  Newspaper & Magazines – inserts
  Yellow pages – Directories
  Door to door
  Word of mouth
  Reputation

D18 How are you going to sell?
- Visit? Phone? or Other?

D19 How will you get your product to the customer? Will...
- They collect?
- You deliver?
- Something else?

BARRIERS

D20 What is to stop you getting into the market?
- Competitors
- Regulations
- Logistics?
- Technology
- Funds

E – THE COMPETITION

YOUR COMPETITORS

E1 Who are they?

E2 What products do they offer?
- Obtain competitor's product sales literature

E3 Are they in essentially the same product/market area you propose?
- If not why not?

E4 If it is the case, why are they not competitors?
- In your product line?
- In your geographic area?

WHAT HAVE THEY SEEN THAT YOU HAVE MISSED?
WHAT HAVE THEY SEEN THAT THEY HAVE MISSED?

E5 Who are their customers?
- Are they happy with the current product(s)? – Will you be able to attract any of them?
  Why?
  How?
  Why not?

E6 What do your potential customers think of your competitors?
- General Reputation
- Price, Quality
- Technology, Delivery
- Pricing Policies – Flexible or fixed
- After sales service
- Operational use
  HOW DO YOU KNOW?

E7 How do they attract their customers?
- How will you beat them?

E8 How do their products compare with those you will offer the customer?
- Delivery, Price
- Pricing policies – flexible or fixed
- After sales service
- Quality
- Technology
- Operational use

E9 How long have they been in the market? – Are they established?
- Well known?
- Good reputation?
- 'Tiger' or 'Lambs'?

E10 How have they dealt with changes in market demand? By:
- Product diversification?
- Price changes?
- Changes in terms of trade?
- Product changes?
- Increase/decrease in quality?
- Changed rate of production?

E11 What are the strengths of their products?
- Design
- Price and quality
- Weight, Size, Colour
- Delivery
- Technology
- After sales service
- Experience
- Ease use

E12 What are the weaknesses of their products?

E13 How do your products compare?
- Design
  Weight
  Size
  Colour
- Price and quality
- Delivery

- Technology
- After sales service
- Experience
- Ease use

E14 Are they financially strong – can they sustain a price war with you, and vice versa?

E15 What will be the natural reaction of your competitors to you entering the market?
- What actions will they take?
  Reduce price?
  Increase production?
  Damage your reputation
  In the eyes of your
  Potential / actual customers?
  Change design
  How will you counter their actions?

E16 Are they growing in size or static or getting smaller?
- Why?

E17 Are they developing their products along the same lines as you?
- If not, why not?

E18 Are their products patented or other-wise protected?
- Are you going to breach them in anyway?

F – PRODUCTION

SUPPLIERS
F1 Are your supplies special or general?

F2 Will you have any single source suppliers?

F2 Will you have any single-source suppliers?
- Who are they?
- How will you protect yourself against:
  Price hikes?
  Delivery Failure?
  Poor standards of quality?

F3 Are your single source or main suppliers financially sound?
- If not, and one fails, how will you protect yourself?

F4 Do your suppliers have to meet specific standards?
- Which?
  How will you ensure compliance'?

F5 Is delivery vital to you?
- How will you protect yourself against failure? Or late delivery?

F6 Is quality vital to you?
- How will you protect yourself against failure? Or failing standards?

F7 Is cost vital to you?
- How will you protect yourself against increases?

MANUFACTURE
F8 Are you going to make, assemble or subcontract?

F9 What special acts and regulations are you going to have to comply with?

F10 What capacity do you need?

F11 What production costs are there?
- Parts and materials, Packing
- Labour, Consumables

F12 What stocks do you need to hold?
- Raw materials and packing
- Finish Goods
- Parts
- After sales service stocks

F13 What are the technical aspects of manufacture?
- Difficulty, Speed
- Quality, Precision
- Heat
- Testing
- Environment

F14 What equipment do you need?
- Production
- Testing / Storing

G – TECHNICAL MATTERS

G1 Is the product fully developed?

G2 What has to be done to complete the development?

G3 How much will it cost to complete the development?

G4 What risks are attached to completion?
- That it won't / can't be completed?
- That it won't be completed soon?

G5 Is this a new area of technology
- What are the perceived risks?
- How are you going to protect yourself against the risks?
- How are your competitors dealing with this technology?

G6 Is this an area of fast technical change?
- How are your competitors dealing with the rate of change?

G7 Where is the technology leading?

G8 Do you need to spend money to maintain product development?
- When?
- How much?

G9 What are the next stages of development?
- How?
- When?

H - LOGISTICS MANAGEMENT

H1 Are you considering going into business with others'?
- As partner(s) or directors?
- With employees?

H2 Who will manage the business?
- When you are away (ill, holiday)?

H3 How will responsibilities be agreed?

PREMISES

Location may be a key factor in the success of the business.

H4 What size of premises do you need?

H5 Do you have to think at the outset about expansion?
- Planning requirement?

H6 Where are you going to operate from?
- Home – possible restrictions of parking
Mortgage company or lease
Visitors – health and safety - Planning permission, change of use?
Visitors - health and safety
Insurance considerations
Tax implications
Noise
Rented premises, purchased property
Shared Property

H7 For EACH of the points above consider also:
- Transport considerations
Availability of supplies
- Labour availability
security – equipment, stock
- The nature of the customer
- passing trade – by foot – by transport – parking – used to delivery

H8 Special needs of the employees?
- Canteen?
- Parking?
- Health & Safety?

EQUIPMENT

H9 What do you need in the way of office equipment?
- Desks, chairs, filing, cupboards
- Computer, printer
- Special – e.g. design boards

H10 What do you need in the way of transport?

SKILLS AND EFFORT

H11 What skills do you need? Consider:

- Marketing and selling
  Financial and accounting
- Legal
  Secretarial and typing
- Production
  Technical

H12 Can you obtain the required skills?

- How?
- Recruitment?
- Full time?
- Part time?
- Friends and relatives?
- Consultants?
- In the proposed locality?
- At affordable costs?
- Easy employee travel?

H13 Is competition for the skills

- Strong – average – weak?

I – RISKS

I1 What are the main risks to your business? Consider:

- Lack of demand
- Competition's product very strong
- Supplier problems
  Delivery
  Quality
  Price
- Manufacturing problems
- Machinery problems
- Technical
  Not completing the product development
  Product obsolescence
  Skills
- Difficult to find expertise
- Personal limitations
- Lack of experience
- Lack of finance
- Matters outside your control
  Economy
  Legislation

I2 What are you going to do to minimise EACH of them?

WHAT TO DO NEXT

That completes the basic questions that you have to tackle and as you start to answer them others will come to mind.

Having now read the questions for a first time:

Have a second brainstorming session, continuing on the same sheets from where you left off.

Don't check to see if you have already made a point in the first session – just keep writing!

Section Two
SO YOU WANT TO START A BUSINESS

IS IT RIGHT FOR YOU?

Contents
Section Two

PART A - WHAT TYPE OF BUSINESS?

INTRODUCTION

As we asked earlier, what type of business do you want to run?

You have three main alternatives:

- **Starting to build your own business from scratch, perhaps with a partner**
- **Buying an existing business other than a franchise**
- **Buy a franchise**

Whichever route you eventually take you will almost certainly have to develop a business plan to determine income, costs, funding and general business viability – certainly if you decide on one of the first two options.

However, we first want to make just a few specific comments on franchises and the purchasing of a business.

FRANCHISES

A franchise is a means whereby a successful company, the franchiser, expands its business by selling its experience and reputation to an individual(s), the franchisee(s).

It is in effect a ready-made business in which the franchisee purchases for a cash investment from the franchiser the right to operate a particular type of business. This business may provide either a product or service.

The cost of a franchise can be substantial if, for example, the business is a profitable household name such as Kentucky Fried Chicken.

KEY POINTS

- You will usually own the business assets such as premises and equipment but some franchisers prefer to lease them.
- You will NEVER own the product name or service or process
- You can usually trade either as an individual, partnership or limited company
- You will not be able to impose your own personal imprint or image on the business
- Your operation and financial results will be under the close scrutiny of the franchiser
- You are very likely to own the franchise for a period of time only – often five years – with only a possible right to renew
- You may have to pay a continuing service cost as well as the initial capital sum
- The service cost may be based on sales
- Just as you will want to vet closely the franchiser so will you be vetted; the franchiser has a reputation to maintain!
- In vetting the franchiser consider:
  his financial viability
  how long has he been selling franchises
  how many franchises he has sold
  if he is a member of the British Franchise Association
  the costs and fees involved
  his outgoing commitment to and relationship with you
- Because you are purchasing (we assume) an established business with a track record, banks are

usually more amenable to lending towards the capital cost – you will still have to raise from your own sources something like a third of the total

- You will be provided with a detailed operations manual and accounting system both of which you will have to stick to (if you are not given them question why not)
- A successful franchise must be a good business idea backed by proper training, promotion and organisation
- Beware! – there are less than scrupulous franchisers about who charge high capital sums without providing training, promotion and organisation
- A reputable franchiser will be willing to provide a list of his franchise for you to talk to about their experience - be on guard if access is denied

Finally ask yourself – "if the business idea is a good as all that why is the franchiser not running the business himself – is selling the franchises the business"?

This does not have to be a problem – just keep it in mind.

A franchise may be a very good proposition but you will always be the junior partner in the business arrangement, taking most, if not all, of the financial risk. You may also be dominated by 'big brother's' control techniques.

✻ ✻ ✻ ✻ ✻ ✻ ✻ ✻

WHAT TO DO NOW

There are seven main steps to purchasing a franchise:

- Research the possible business areas – obtain a copy of the United Kingdom Franchise Directory for an outline of the industry, general information and details of some of the 1000 franchise opportunities
- Go to one of the several franchise exhibitions
- Read the magazine *Franchiseworld*
- Draw up your short list and send for details
- Visit the potential franchisers
- Obtain independent advice
- Contact existing franchisees fro their experience
- Organise finance – most banks have specialist departments
- Sign up

ADDITIONALLY:

- Read one of the several books on the market providing detailed information on this type of venture
- Refer to the British Franchise Association for advice
- **Always seek professional advice from a solicitor specialising in Franchise contracts – they are special.**
- **Have an accountant work with the solicitor on reviewing the financial aspects, especially your tax status related to the legal form in which you expect to trade.**

BUYING A BUSINESS

Buying a business is even more problematic than the purchase of a franchise because the variable factors and unknowns are usually greater.

As in the case of a franchise there will likely be an initial capital sum to pay, but whereas this may be fairly well ascertained in the case of a franchise, the first problem in a company purchase will be to establish:

- Exactly what you are purchasing
- What amount to pay for it

The price for the business will divide in most cases into three parts:

- Fixed assets – those thing you can see and touch such as building, equipment, furniture and fittings
- Trading assets – stocks and work in progress, debtors, bank and cash, creditors
- Those assets which have value but which you cannot see – intangible assets – such as patent, specialised technical human skills and other expertise, a lease, goodwill

How a business is valued can be complicated and requires specialised experience; the intangible assets, particularly goodwill, may be the most difficult of all. In essence, this is the extra amount you are prepared to pay over and above the value of the other two parts to obtain the business.

For example, the asking purchase price of a small retail business may divide as follows:

Freehold, premises, fixtures......£70,000
Net working capital stock,
debtors, Bank, creditors............£15,000
Goodwill......................................£30,000
£115,000

Your advisors may agree with 'the other side' after investigation and negotiation that the first two items can be settled at £75,000, but what about the extra?

The goodwill represents what the vendor believes you should pay now for the profits you are going to make in the future as a result of his past efforts in building the business – the site is a good one with a lot of passing trade and parking, the business has a good reputation in the area, it has a solid customer base and so on.

You will want to have the amount reduced and an important part of your financial advisor's role will be to review past financial results in depth and to make an assessment of future profitability.

A ratio will then be struck in terms of how many years' profits are covered in the asked – for value of goodwill. For example, if profits are forecast to be £10,000 a year you are in effect paying for three year's profits (if you settle for £30,000) – the more years you pay for the more expensive the charge for goodwill.

Negotiation becomes a 'haggle' – how much do you want the business? – How much does the vendor want to, or have to, sell for a lower value?

And there is much, much more:

- Dealing with contracts and leases of existing customers and landlords
- Determining how strong the business really is
- Determining how sound the customer base and reputation really is
- What has to be done in terms of re-equipping and modernising the business
- Perhaps negotiating planning permissions, especially if there is a change of use of premises

Finally there are the up-front costs to cover the fees of accountants and solicitors to investigate the business, as well as time and effort on negotiations and related matters – all of which may come to nought if you don't proceed to purchase the business.

This can be the right way to get into business but it is formal and needs thought.

WHAT TO DO NOW

- If it is a serious consideration you should read one of the many excellent books on the market so that you have an understanding of what will be involved.
- Choose your potential business and location – there are many newspapers and magazines that provide details of businesses for sale
- Consider trade magazines – for example, hotel and catering magazines, if you are looking for a restaurant or hotel
- Even although your accountant will have been through the financial affairs of the target business you will need a business plan covering the near-term future, and you will be a key player in its preparation; if you need to borrow money there will be no avoiding it.
- **You must seek experienced financial and legal advice on this matter – it cannot be done without it.**

STARTING FROM SCRATCH

One of the main drawbacks to buying a franchise or existing business is just that, the 'buying' and formalities and the capital cost involved and an alternative for many people will be to start from scratch.

This is often the route for those who have a skill or experience they want to build on and if you have been through Part One you will be aware of many of the 'pros and cons'. Others include:

- The need for little or no capital to start with (perhaps)
- Comparative lack of complexity and difficulty

- The lack of formidable commitment and obligation that comes with the hard and defined start of purchasing a business, perhaps with responsibility for employees – in other words, you can 'slip into it' or research it while you care still employed.

WHAT TO DO NOW

- Think about your business idea if you have one and compare it to the other options we have briefly considered
- Talk to others who have started from nothing
- Talk to others who have bought a franchise or business
- Pursue your idea, through the early stages of writing a business plan

Whichever route you decide to venture you will certainly have to do some planning . . . so read on.

PLANNING CONSIDERATIONS CREATING A SUCCESSFUL BUSINESS

There are three key stages in creating a successful business:

- Defining the business in a plan
- Preparing the activity plan – the 'make it happen' plan – the planning stage of starting a business, the key elements of which are often part of the business plan.
- Doing it!

Which is more important is hard to say, certainly of the first two, and all should be regarded as parts of an integrated whole; an architect (or any designer for that matter, cars, aircraft, trains) may design the finest concert hall but his efforts will be to nought without good planners and organisers – and the builders cannot do it without those plans and supervision.

BUT

Our experience tells us, time and time again, that the more work that foes into a business before its launch the better it will work afterwards.

PLANNING

There is nothing magical about planning, and a business plan is simply a written explanation of what your business is all about, how it will work and why it will be successful.

Such a plan has three purposes:

- To act as a process of clarification of the concepts involved. A guide is that:

If you cannot produce a clear written explanation of your proposed business, in particular the financial aspects, you do not understand that business.

- To provide a basis for deciding whether or not to go ahead
- To explain to potential investors why they should lend money to the business, the risks involved and the profit they will earn from the investment

Its length can be as short or as long as is necessary to meet the above needs; in general terms the greater:

- The complexity of the business

And/or

- The amount of investment

And/or

- The risks of failure

The longer and more involved will be the business plan.

The period to be covered will be decided by the complexity of the case, the life of any underlying project and the length of time needed to archive financial viability.

In general terms it should at least cover the formative period to when the business can be regarded as financially established.

The contents of a plan essentially hand round the following skeleton:

- A summary
- although it comes first it can only sensibly be written LAST; it provided the reader with a clear idea of the key features of the business and its future financial results
- The body of the plan
- Which provides all the main substance and justifications
- The conclusion
- The appendices
- Where necessary the detailed evidence for the points made in the body of the plan and **always include the detailed financial information.**

INTRODUCING FINANCIAL FORECASTS

What about forecasts and finance? – They are, or course integral to the planning process and we consider the subject again later in **Financial Forecasting.**

Financial forecasts paint a picture, reflecting in money terms the real things that happen in a business:

- Products are made by people (wages and salaries) from parts and materials (purchases) bought from suppliers. Often you will owe money to them (creditors, people, even if they do want your money!)
- Customers are real people who buy your products (sales) – if they don't pay straight away they are your debtors
- You may work from or with building, plant, equipment and transport (fixed or leased assets)

- And with luck you will end with money in your bank (black bank balance)

Your financial forecast represents a real, living business and, as we said earlier, if you cannot prepare one that stands up to detailed scrutiny you don't know your business.

The financial information must always be the narrative plan presented in money values; thus if the plan talks in term of sales rising by 5% per annum the figures must also show this.

✽ ✽ ✽ ✽ ✽ ✽ ✽ ✽

Financial plans normally include:
- The cash flows
- The profit and loss flows
- The balance sheets
- The assumptions on which the figures are based
- Supporting details, evidence and calculation

Financial forecasting can be daunting to many people – in particular, the concept behind the profit and loss account and balance sheet can be difficult to grasp.

You will need financial advice on a range of matters, and assistance with preparing the detailed financial forecasts should be part of this. Nevertheless, it is not difficult to prepare a cash flow forecast and you should gather financial data as you work through the exercise, for example on:
- The cost of equipment you will have to buy
- The cost of supplies and purchase
- The cost of rented premises and other related charges

We provide examples of a number of common items of income and expenditure later in **Financial Forecasting** that will act as mid-joggers.

✽ ✽ ✽ ✽ ✽ ✽ ✽ ✽

ACTIVITY PLANNING

But **financial forecasting** is only the story – you also need plans to 'make it happen' another part of business planning.

Activity planning need only match the complexity of the proposed business and may consist of a number of levels, demonstrated in the following example related to the purchase of a shop to sell carpets. Simply put, it is the steps you have to go through, rather than the money forecasting or narrative explanation.

LEVEL 1 – TOP LEVEL TIMETABLE Month	1	2	3	4	5	6	7
A – Choose shop (plan 2A	x	x					
B – Agree terms and lease			x	x			
C – Agree and order fittings				x	x		
D – Advertise				x	x	x	
E – Order and receive stock					x	x	
F – Open for business							x

LEVEL 2 – PLAN 2a – CHOOSING THE SHOP Weeks	1	2	3	4	5	6	7
A – Agree possible location(s)	x						
B – Visit location(s)		x	x				
C – Decide on area and consider potential shops				x	x		
D – Make initial approaches					x	x	
E – Start to negotiate					x		x

You may find it quite difficult to piece the business plan together In the early stages, in particular the financial aspects, without doing some activity planning.

For example, how would you in the above example know when you could start trading or from when rent, heating, lighting and so on might become payable without going through the simple planning stages.

We bring this into the work exercise.

HOW TO APPROACH YOUR PLANNING TASK

We have said that all aspects of a business are interrelated; as you investigate one area other questions come to mind and revision is needed to earlier ideas – you cannot simply work through this exercise in one sweep, so to speak.

To help you round this problem we:
- Start by giving you the questions you are going to answer – Basic Questions

and
- When you have completed your research we take you though the preparation of your business plan

Basic Questions is a comprehensive set of points to consider and you will have to be selective in:
- Choosing those questions you need to answer
- And the depth of research you undertake in answering them

A window cleaner will not need as much detailed thought as someone looking to set up a car repair service or a building business.

But remember that this is your business-you want it to work – it is your livelihood – and you should do whatever is needed to maximise the chances of making it a success and minimising the risk of failure.

Whatever the complexity and depth . . . you must check your assumptions wherever possible.

Too much Business Planning is based on beliefs that are never checked ~ as such they remain beliefs rather than a considered position and will almost certainly be unreliable.

You will always need to apply judgement and experience ~ but apply it to as sound and as factual a basis as possible. Except in a few isolated cases you can never be certain that your assumptions are correct ~ Disneyland! ~ but you can also take all practical steps to verify them wherever possible.

Continually ask yourself: HOW YOU KNOW?

Just to remind you we insert the question every now and again as we go through the 'basic questions'.

What to do now:

The following tips may be useful:

- Open and maintain an arch-lever working file on which to keep details of all your research and ideas – we provide one or two formats at the end of the book to start you off – you will be referred to them as and when...

- We have referenced the points in BASIC QUESTIONS and suggest that you keep a separate working sheet(s) for each answer

- As you do your research and matters come to mind keep a record of the activities you will have to undertake as part of the activity plan – we come back to this

- We suggest that you first work through the points without worrying too much about the financial aspects – first get the idea clear and what has to be done; again we come back to this point

- If you have more than one idea to research start a separate file – DO NOT MIX YOUR INFORMATION

✳ ✳ ✳ ✳ ✳ ✳ ✳ ✳ ✳

YOUR BASIC CONCEPT

Enough reading – now for some doing!

Before you tackle the BASIC QUESTIONS in PART B, we would like you to prepare a simple statement of your business concept.

GO TO APPENDIX A and NOTE THE NATURE OF YOUR BUSINESS IDEA AS CLEARLY AS POSSIBLE

Do not turn this page until you have done this exercise.

DID YOU FIND IT EASY TO DESCRIBE YOUR BUSINESS?

It may not be quiet as simple as you first thought. Suppose you want to start an electrical appliance business – your first statement may have been just as simple as:

TO RUN AN ELECTRICAL APPLIANCE REPAIR BUSINESS

On the face of it the proposition seems OK but in fact it is imprecise and leaves a number of unanswered questions!

Business is concerned with supplying goods and services that meet the needs of customers:

- Industrial or private business?
- What appliances? All appliances? – irons and/or clothes washing machines and/or dishwashers and/or kettles and/or fridges and/or cookers and/or TVs and/or hairdryers, and so on
- What makes of appliances? – UK and/or services? – Particular suppliers?
- When is the service available? – 24 hour/ 7 days a week / bank holidays – Christmas day?
- Where? – local town – within 30 minutes drive – region ?
- How? Appliance brought to you or you go to it?
- How quickly? – Within 24 hours – shorter/longer?

In this case, therefore, the first statement might be revised after short consideration to:

- Start a business
- Running it initially from home
- Offering a repair service for UK manufactured, domestic washing machines, dishwashers, and clothes driers
- At a customer's premises within an hour's drive

- During the hours 8am to 6pm, six days a week, excluding bank holidays

We will come back to your concept later on but bearing in mind our comments above, do you want to refine your first draft? – Before we really get down to it!

If so go to appendix A1 and prepare a second statement – be precise and stick to the bullet points we have provided.

WHAT TO DO NOW

- We want you to have a 'brainstorming' session on all the various things you think you are going to have to plan to get your business off the ground – in other words, a first session on activity planning
- Find somewhere quiet and simply note down EVERYTHING that comes to mind IN ANY ORDER just as it flows from the mind – JUST WRITE! Spend as long on the task as you wish – or until your thoughts run dry!

APPENDIX B is the sheet to get you started but you will certainly need more.

When you have finished this, put the exercises you have done to date on the working paper file and when ready, move to the next chapter.

PART B - BASIC QUESTIONS

INTRODUCTION

We now give the questions we want you to consider, research and answer. They are split into the following groups:

- The purpose and goals of the business
- The product
- Your customers
- The market
- The competition
- Production
- Technical
- Logistics
- Risks

As we said earlier, some may not be entirely appropriate – only you can decide – but you should have a very good reason for not answering a question.

To save repeating ourselves, where we use the term 'product' you should also take this to mean 'service' or a combination of product and service, whichever is the appropriate meaning.

First, read Part B through to the end of 'Risks' to get a feel for the task ahead, before you start to answer the points ~ then continue on to 'What to do next'.

A – THE PURPOSE AND GOALS OF YOUR BUSINESS

A business has to have a purpose – this is not the same as describing the basic business concept.

A1 What is the purpose of the business – simply to provide sufficient income for you, or to grow into something else?

- To provide employment to/for:
- To be a business that...by
- To be the largest
  the only
  the most
  the best

A2 What are the goals of the business on the way to achieving its purpose? There may be several of them.

- To dominate the chosen market
- To secure a percentage of the chosen market
- To earn profits of....
- Customer satisfaction
- Customer loyalty
- To take over....
- To develop products to...

A3 How are you going to measure whether or not you achieve the goals? How are you going to measure success?

B – THE PRODUCT

There are two matters of almost equal importance – the product you are proposing to offer and the customers who will buy your product – and you cannot really separate the two – together they define the market you are in.

B1 What are you offering?
- Is it a service?
  Relying on your skill and experience?
  How can it be developed?
- Is it a product?
  A material object
  How can it be developed?
- Is it a combination of the two?
  How can it be developed?

B2 What are the key elements of your product?
- Is it a new idea, something not thought of before?
- Is it easy to copy?
- Can it be easily replaced by another product
- Should it be patented
- Is it a quick gimmick, a one off?
- Is it doing better something that is already available?
- Is it doing cheaper something that is already available?

B3 What makes your product different from others on the market?
- What is its unique selling feature(s)?

B4 What are the benefits of the product to the customer?

HOW DO YOU KNOW?

B5 What are the strengths of the product?
- How are you going to build on them?

B6 What are the weaknesses of the product?
- How are you going to eliminate them?

B7 Does your product meet the needs of the customer?

HOW DO YOU KNOW?

C – YOUR CUSTOMERS

C1 Who are your customers?

C2 Are there groups of customers?
- With different likelihoods of taking your products
- Strong, good, fair & poor chance?

C3 What is the profile (description of a typical customer or group?

C4 What are their requirements and needs?
- What is the most important thing to them?

HOW DO YOU KNOW?

C5 How are you sure their needs are not already being satisfied?

C6 What influences your customer to buy or not to buy?

C7 What are the dissatisfaction factors of customer?

C8 How loyal are they likely to be to their current suppliers?

C9 How are customer needs and requirements going to change?

C10 What alternative sources of supply do your customers have (to you)?

IN SHORT

Why should a customer buy from you rather than your competitors?

Why should they part with their money to you?

D – THE MARKET PLACE
(You should also refer to Appendix C – Marketing)

SIZE

D1 What has been the recent history of the market?

D2 Is the market static in size?
- Are you going to be fighting for market share or part of an increasing market?

D3 What affects the rate of change in market size?

D4 Are your customers all in one trade sector or is there demand in others?

D5 How are you going to make the market grow, or your share of it?

D6 What market research already exists in this field?

DEMAND

D7 Is demand:
For the product
- Increasing?
- Decreasing? } And why?
- Static?

In the area
- Increasing?
- Decreasing? } And why?
- Static?

D8 What affects demand for the product? Consider:
- Economic conditions
- Cyclical
- Are you entering at the right time?
- Employment/Unemployment levels
- Environment
- Pollution
- Fashion and Style
- Will product become out of date quickly?

- Technical Development
- Will product become out of date quickly?
- Weather
  Outdoor activities
  Seasonal Matters
- Regulations or lack of them
- Competition
  Delivery, response time
  Price
- Quality
- After sales service
- Location
- Status of customer
- Spending power
- Married / single / divorced / family
- Sex of customer
- Car Owner
- Home Owner
- Age
- Education
- Qualification
- Social Class
- General Lifestyle
- Health
- Eating and drinking habits
- Status of general population
- Spending Power
- Married / Single / divorced / family
- Car owner
- Home owner
- Age
- Education
- Social Class
- General Lifestyle
- Health
- Eating and drinking habits
- Exercise habits
- How often the customer needs to buy the products – day of the week, time in the month, once a year?
- Is the product a need or a luxury?
- Is the product related to the demand for other products/ services?

- Religion
- Ethnic and national origin
- Politics
- Convenience

D9 How will you cope with a falling demand?

- Change of product?
- Move into a different line of business?
- Reduce price?

D10 How will you cope with an increase in demand?

- Increase production?
- Expand?
- Increase price?

D11 How big is the market in terms of:

- Spending power?
- Area?
- Number of customer?
- Number of Suppliers?

D12 How quickly will the demand for your product build up?

D13 What makes you believe there is room for another supplier in the market – YOU?

PRICE

D14 What is the current range of prices?

- What causes the difference?

D15 What price will the market stand?

- How do customers view price?
- What is the product worth to the customer?
- How do your competitors price their product?
- Is price 'elastic'?
- If you change the price a little will demand change a lot?

- If you change the price a lot will the demand stay much the same?

HOW DO YOU KNOW?

D16 How are you going to price your product?

- Will customers be suspicious of quality if it is too low?

SELLING

D17 How are you going to attract your customers?

- Advertising
- Newspapers and magazines
- Inserts
- Yellow Pages
- Directories
- Door to door
- Word of mouth
- Reputation

D18 How are you going to sell?

- Visit?
- Phone?

D19 How will you get your product to the customer?

- They collect?
- You deliver?
- Someone Else?

BARRIERS

D20 What is to stop you getting into the market?

- Competitors?
- Regulations?
- Logistics?
- Technology?
- Expertise?
- Funds?
- How will you overcome them?

E – THE COMPETITION

Use the format in Appendix D to build up a picture of each of your competitors.

COMPETITORS

E1 Who are they?

E2 What Products do they offer?
- Obtain competitors product sales literature

E3 Are they in essentially the same product/market area you propose?
- If not why not?

E4 If it is the case, why are there no competitors?
- In your product line?
- In your geographic area?
- **WHAT HAVE THEY SEEN THAT YOU HAVE MISSED?**
- **WHAT HAVE YOU SEEN THAT THEY HAVE MISSED?**

E5 Who are their customers?
- Are they happy with the current product(s)?
- Will you be able to attract any of them?
- Why?
- How?
- Why not?

E6 What do your potential customers think of your competitors?
- General Reputation
- Delivery
- Price
- Pricing policies
- Flexible or fixed
- Quality
- After sales service
- Technology
- Operational use

HOW DO YOU KNOW?

E7 How do they attract their customers?
- How will you beat them?

E8 How do their products compare with those you will offer regarding the needs of the customer?
- Delivery
- Price
- Pricing policies
- Flexible or fixed
- Quality
- After sales service
- Technology
- Operational use

E9 How long have they been in the market?
- Are they established?
- Well known?
- Good reputation?
- Tigers or lambs?

E10 How have they dealt with changes in market demand? By:
- Product diversification?
- Price changes?
- Changes in terms of trade?
- Product changed?
- An increase / decrease in quality
- Changed rate of production?

E11 What are the strengths of their products?
- Design
- Weight
- Size
- Colour
- Price
- Quality
- Delivery
- Technology

- After sales service
- Experience
- Ease of use

E12 What are the weaknesses of their products?
- Design
- Weight
- Size
- Colour
- Price
- Quality
- Delivery
- Technology
- After sales services
- Experience
- Ease of use

E13 How do your products compare?
- Design
- Weight
- Size
- Colour
- Price
- Quality
- Delivery
- Technology
- After sales service
- Experience
- Ease of us

E14 Are they financially strong – can they sustain a price war with you, and vice versa?

E15 What will be the natural reaction of your competitors to you entering the market?
- What actions will they take?
- Reduce Price?
- Increase production?
- Damage your reputation in the eyes of your potential/actual customers
- Change design
- How will you counter their actions?

E16 Are they growing in size or static or getting smaller?
- Why?

E17 Are they developing their products along the same lines as you?
- If not, why?

E18 Are their products patented or otherwise protected?
- Are you going to breach them in any way?

F – PRODUCTION
SUPPLIERS
F1 Are your supplies special or general?

F2 Will you have any single-source supplies?
- Why are they?
- How will you protect yourself against:-
- Price hikes?
- Delivery failure?
- Poor standards of quality?

F3 Are your single source or main suppliers financially sound?
- If not, and one fails, how will you protect yourself?

F4 Do your supplies (ers) have to meet specific regulations? For example material standards?
- Which?
- How will you ensure compliance?

F5 Is delivery vital to you?
- How will you protect yourself against failure? Or late delivery?

F6 Is quality vital to you?
- How will you protect yourself against failure? Or failing standards?

F7 Is cost vital to you?
- How will you protect yourself against increases?

MANUFACTURE

F8 Are you going to manufacture, assemble or subcontract?

F9 What special acts and regulations are you going to have to comply with?

F10 What capacity do you have?

F11 What productions costs are there?

- Parts and materials
- Packing
- Labour
- Consumables

F12 What stocks do you need to hold?

- Raw materials and packing
- Finished Goods
- Parts
- After sales service stocks

F13 What are the technical aspects of manufacture?

- Difficulty
- Speed
- Quality
- Precision
- Heat
- Testing
- Environment

F14 What equipment do you need?

- Production
- Testing
- Storing

G – TECHNICAL MATTERS

G1 Is the product fully developed?

G2 What has to be done to complete the development?

G3 How much will it cost to complete the development?

G4 What risks are attached to the competition? That is:

- that it won't/can't be completed?
- that it won't be completed soon enough?

G5 Is this a new area of technology?

- what are the perceived risks?
- how are you going to protect yourself against the risks?
- how are you going to protect yourself against the risks?
- how are your competitors dealing with this technology?

G6 Is this an area of fast technical change?

- how are your competitors dealing with the rate of change?

G7 Where is the technology leading?

G8 Do you need to spend money to maintain product development?

- when?
- how much?

G9 What are the next stages of development?

- how?
- when?

H – LOGISTICS

MANAGEMENT

H1 Are you considering going into business with others?

- As partner(s) or directors?
- With employees?

H2 Who will manage the business?

- When you are away (I'll, holiday)

H3 How will responsibilities be agreed?

PREMISES

Location may be a key factor in the success of the business.

H4 What size of premises do you need?

H5 Do you have to think at the outset about expansion?

- Planning requirement

H6 Where are you going to operate from?

- Home
- Restrictions of mortgage company or lease
- Planning permission, change of use
- Visitors – health and safety – parking
- Insurance considerations
- Noise
- Rented Premises
- Purchased property
- Shared Property

H7 For EACH of the points above consider also:

- Transport considerations
- Availability of supplies
- Labour availability
- Security – equipment, stock
- The nature of the customer
- Passing trade

- By foot
- By transport
- Parking
- Used to delivery

H8 Special needs of the employees?

- Canteen
- Parking
- Health & Safety

EQUIPMENT

H9 What do you need in the way of office equipment?

- Desks, chairs, filling, cupboards
- Computer, Printer
- Special – design boards

H10 What do you need in the way of transport?

SKILLS AND EFFORT

H11 What skills do you need? Consider:

- Marketing & Selling
- Financial and accounting
- Legal
- Secretarial and typing
- Production
- Technical

H12 Can you obtain the required skills?

- How?
- Recruitment
- Full time
- Part time
- Friends and relatives
- Consultants
- In the proposed locality?
- At affordable costs
- Easy employee Travel

H13 Is competition for the skills:

- Strong – average - weak?

I – RISKS

I1 What are the main risks to your business? Consider:

- Lack of demand
- Competitions products very strong
- Supplier problems
- Delivery
- Quality
- Price
- Manufacturing problems
- Machinery problems
- Technical
- Not completing the product development
- Product obsolescence
- Skills
- Difficult to find expertise
- Personal Limitations
- Lack of experience
- Lack of finance
- Matters outside your control
- Economy
- Legislation

I2 What are you going to do to minimise EACH of them?

WHAT TO DO NEXT

That completes the basic questions that you have to tackle and as you start to answer them others will come to mind.

Having now read the questions for a first time:

- **Have a second 'Brainstorming' session, continuing on the same sheets from where you left off . . .**

  Don't check to see if you have already made a point in the first session – just keep writing!

When you have completed the second session we would like you to review all the points you have made; you will notice that they fall naturally into groupies, for example, product, competitors, equipment, development, administration and so on.

PLEASE CREATE A NEW SHEET OF PAPER FOR EACH GROUP.

- Enter each item on the appropriate group sheet:
- NOW eliminating any duplicate entries
- Where possible placing them in order of timing, i.e., earliest items first in terms of needing to do
- Leaving a reasonable space between each item to add further related items as you think of them later on

As you enter each item try and think of at least one or two more activities related to that item. For example, you may have a group title called GENERAL ADMIN, and one of the items in your brainstorm may have been 'stationery'

As you enter the item 'stationery' under the group called GENERAL ADMIN think of other matters that relate to 'stationery'. :

GENERAL ADMIN

- Stationery
  - Letterhead
    Style, Colour
      Legal requirements
  - Calling cards
    Style, Colour
      Legal requirements
  - Invoices
  - Pre-Printed Envelopes

In this way you will have started to build up a considerable number of points to help you with your activity planning, and the sessions will have been a useful exercise in starting to think about your business.

When you have finished this grouping exercise you will be ready to research the answers to the questions we gave in BASIC QUESTIONS so please turn to the next section.

YOUR RESEARCH

Having got this far you will be anxious to get on with the detailed examination of your idea but you will be surprised how much of it is already fitting into place; by now you will:

- Have a reasonably clear idea of the definition of your business
- Have an understanding of the questions you need to answer
- Have had a first stab at identifying the activities you will need to tackle

From here on it is up to you for a while. You must

- Work in a methodical fashion
- Determine what you want to tackle first
- Keep ALL (throw nothing away) your information in a sensible and orderly manner on the arch-lever work file:
- Keep separate sections for each section of your investigation, for example:

  Business concept statements

  Brainstorming results

  Answers to the BASIC QUESTIONS

  The business plan

  The activity plans

  The financial forecasts

- If not already done place on the file work completed

  The statements on business concept

  The group sheets prepared from your brainstorming sessions and the original sheets
- Not be tempted to move to the drafting stage of the plan until you have done your research
- Keep a separate section fro financial matters; consider the types of expenditure you may need to collect, many of which we list in FINANCIAL FORECASTING; make a list of the terms and a record of them as the information comes to hand
- **As you answer the BASIC QUESTIONS add other points to the activity grouping lists that come to mind**

What to do now?

DO YOUR RESEARCH

PART C - THE BUSINESS PLAN

You will eventually reach the point where you want to prepare the first draft of your business plan.

I am shortly going to take you through a format that will be a suitable basis for many, if not most business ideas.

THE STATEMENT OF BUSINESS CONCEPT

Firstly I want you to go back, having done your homework, to your revised business concept to see if it has changed.

CONSIDER THE TWO DRAFTS ALREADY DONE AND IN THE LIGHT OF YOUR SUBSEQUENT THINKING, PREPARE THE FINAL VIEW OF YOUR BUSINESS IDEA. DO IT ON APPENDIX A2.

Same rules - short, clear points, please!

✻✻✻✻✻✻✻✻✻

TWO NEW EXERCISES

There are two other detailed' matters to clarify:

As separate exercises, please CLEARLY, in BULLET POINT FORM (Short points of a few words only):

1. Define what are the aims of the business
2. Describe:
   - 2.1 The products
   - 2.2 The benefits to the customer

When you have done this you will have a clear idea of:

- Your business idea
- The product or service you wish to offer
- The benefits to the customerAnd you will be a long way through your activity planning!

YOU HAVE NOW COMPLETED A LOT OF WORK!

THE BUSINESS PLAN ITSELF

INTRODUCTION TO THE PLAN

OK? – Now to the plan!

To recap, the first step in creating a successful business is the planning stage and the key part of this is the business plan. We have said that the first purpose of the plan is:

- To act as a process of clarification of the concepts involved. A fundamental rule is:

IF YOU CANNOT PRODUCE A CLEAR WRITTEN EXPLANATION OF YOUR PROPOSED BUSINESS, IN PARTICULAR THE FINANCIAL ASPECTS, YOU DO NOT UNDERSTAND THAT BUSINESS

Or in other words you must be able to state clearly:

- WHAT YOUR BUSINESS IS
- HOW IT IS GOING TO WORK
- WHY IT WILL BE SUCCESSFUL
- THE POTENTIAL FINANCIAL RESULTS

It must:

- SOUND AN ATTRACTIVE PROPOSAL
- BE CREDIBLE
- BE ACHIEVABLE

Also remember that it is YOUR PLAN, NOT YOUR ADVISOR'S PLAN:

- YOU must understand it
- YOU must be able to talk it through and explain it
- YOU MUST BELIEVE IT

YOU, after all, are going to have to run the business!

What follows is the wording that might start a particular topic included in a plan. We emphasise that this can only be an indication of the approach, and what and how much is actually included will depend on each particular case. It will give you, however, a good idea of what it's all about.

Remember – That an investor or other lender will want as much evidence as possible for what you are saying and the assumptions you are relying on.

WHAT SHOULD YOU DO NOW?

- Read through the outline wording I have given to get a feel of it and then, bearing in mind what I said above, decide on the contents of your plan
- There may be some timing points that cannot be finally agreed until you have prepared the activity plans – don't worry about this
- Don't worry about the activity plans or financial forecasts at this stage – we will come back to these at a later stage

Remember that:

- Product means not just something of substance but also the provision of a service.
- The words 'I' and 'We' are interchangeable

JUST READ THROUGH THE OUTLINE PLAN AT THE MOMENT

THE PLAN - FRONT PAGE

PROPOSED NAME
BUSINESS PLAN FOR:
(Brief Identification of the venture)
FOR THE PERIOD:
PREPARED BY:
DATE:

THE PLAN – CONTENTS

CONTENTS
THE BUSINESS PLAN
- Summary
- Narrative Plan

APPENDICES
- Activity Plans
- Financial Appendices
  Assumptions
  Cash Flow
  Profit flow
  Balance sheets

THE PLAN – SUMMARY

SUMMARY
The purpose of the SUMMARY is:
- To give the reader a quick and clear understanding of the business proposition
- To make him want to read further

It should be no more than two pages in final narrative from and provide a clear but concise outline of the business proposition; it should include key points only and may be cross-referenced to the business plan details:
- What the business is
- The product
- The market
- The competition
- The risks
- Why the business will succeed
- Required financial investment
- The financial results
- Conclusion

The SUMMARY 'flows from' the NARRATIVE PLAN and it can ONLY be successfully prepared when the rest of the plan is finished.
- DO NOT write THE SUMMARY FIRST
- DO NOT include any information in the SUMMARY that is not referred to, in the narrative section or appendices

THE PLAN – NARRATIVE PLAN

INTRODUCTION

We are proposing to start a . . .

The background to our involvement in this business venture is . . .

The market(s) in which we see this opportunity . . .

(Describe it and its features)

The goals of the business are . . .

We believe the venture will be successful because . . .

The business will be operational by . . .

Assuming that . . .

(Enter key points – funding in place, lease signed)

The key timetable dates are shown in Activity Plan 1, Appendix . . .

THE MARKET

THE PRODUCT

We are proposing to offer . . .

(Describe in detail – if it is technical and/or very detailed include in an appendix)

The features of our product are as follows . . .

(Describe the identifying aspects of the product)

THE MARKET AREA

We are going to operate in the following market(s) . . .

The features of this market(s) are . . .

(Describe the market)

THE CUSTOMERS

Typically our potential customers are . . .

(Describe them)

Their needs are . . .

(Describe them)

They are/are not receiving good service because . . .

Demand for the product is dependent upon . . .

THE COMPETITION

There are . . . competitors in . . .

(Describe here the size and general nature of the competition)

In summary the products they offer include . . . and we provide details of the products they offer in appendix . . .

(Provide a general description of the products in the market place)

In general the strengths are . . .

In general the weaknesses are . . .

THE BENEFITS

The benefits of our product are . . .

These meet the needs of the customer in the following ways . . .

We believe our product has the following advantages over that of our competitors . . .

SALES

We are going to attract our customers by . . .

(Describe how you will advertise or otherwise attract your customers)

We will see the product . . .

(Describe the nature of the provision if the product)

Sales are expected to build over time by . . .

ENTERING THE MARKET

We expect / do not expect the following problems on entering the market . . .

(Describe here the difficulties you anticipate in entering the market (or not as the case may be and how you expect to overcome them)

TECHNICAL ASPECTS

CURRENT PRODUCT DEVELOPMENT

The position on current development is . . .

(This should state the progress made on the current development; if complicated it should be expanded in an appendix)

Current product development will . . .

(Describe the development plan to completion)

We do / do not envisage any difficulties . . .

(State your judgement on the future development giving reasons)

FUTURE PRODUCT DEVELOPMENT

Once the business is established we envisage that we will seek to develop the product along the following lines . . .

Because . . .

(Provide details of market and customer development, technology and other influences)

STRUCTURE OF THE BUSINESS

The senior management team is composed of . . .

(Brief personal details, in particular covering relevant experience; more complex organisations may need CVs in an appendix)

It is proposed that the business will be run as a . . .

(Describe the immediate and future status of the company, sole trader, limited company etc.)

In summary, the organisation at the end of the first year is envisaged to be as follows . . .

See appendix . . . for fuller information

(State simply the management organisation, staffing numbers and other related matters)

The recruitment plan is given in appendix . . .

OPERATIONS

Location

To carry on business we need . . .

(Explain the nature of the premises, need for expansion)

We are going to operate the business from . . . (If known give details)

To do this we are going to have to . . .

(Key steps to moving to premises)

Equipment

We need / do not need any special requirements and details are given in appendix . . . . .

Regarding:

- Item
- Supplier
- Cost
- When needed

(You should provide details of what you need to buy however little)

Production

The production facilities we need are . . .

(Brief description)

And fuller details are provided in appendix . . .

They should be ready for operations by . . .

Employment

The skills we need include . . .

(Describe the types of employment)

Appendix . . . shows how this will be built up through time

These skills are / are not readily available . . .

(Describe the availability of the appropriate skills and / or how you will satisfy the requirements)

RISKS

The business faces the following key risks; we give for each our assessment of its impact on the business and our contingency plans and proposed actions for minimising their effect. (You should consider the risks under each of the headings included in your plan, e.g., the market, technical aspects, structure of the business and so on)

THE MARKET

- Risk:

  How we will counter:
- Risk:

  How we will counter:

FINANCIAL ASSESSMENT

(There will be full analysis of the financial results in the appendices and you should only include here the key points that highlight potential success and funding needs)

Appendix . . . . . provides an analysis of the forecast results from which the following key points are taken:

- The cash flows become positive . . .
- The business becomes profitable in . . .
- The financial results are sensitive in the following way . . .

(Describe here, for example, what happens to cash and profits if sales reduce by given percentages, or build up more slowly then forecast)

- The funding requirements are . . .

(Describe the needs and proposed methods)

CONCLUSION

We believe that sufficient work has been undertaken to demonstrate that:

- We can achieve the goals of the business within the timescale set
- Demand exists for our product
- We can produce and deliver the product at a price, quality and timing that meets the needs of the customer
- We have assessed the risks, understand them and believe know how to deal with them
- Income and costs are such that there is sufficient gross margin to meet the overheads, interest on funding, funding repayments and leave an acceptable level of profit before tax
- The proposed funding requirements will meet the needs of the business
- The financial viability of the business is sound

For these reasons we have to decide to proceed with the venture, subject to . . .

(Detail the qualifying points, e.g., putting funding and legal arrangements in place)

SIGNED ....

DATE ....

SIGNED ....

DATE ....

❋ ❋ ❋ ❋ ❋ ❋ ❋ ❋

The signing process is important – it signifies that you, personally, are 'standing by' what you say in the business plan.

❋ ❋ ❋ ❋ ❋ ❋ ❋ ❋

THE PLAN –
THE APPENDICES

The appendices are an important part of the plan and should complement the narrative section by providing additional detailed information.

If in doubt as to what to include where:

- Keep the information in the narrative section shorted rather than longer. The reader may want a relatively quick understanding and can always refer to the appendices if he needs further details
- The appendices must not include information that is not referred to in the narrative, it they must not include ORIGINAL information
- Include more rather than less information in the appendices
- Include detailed charts, analysis, listing and specifications in the appendices

What you should do now

Having read through the outline you should now start to prepare the draft NARRATIVE SECTION ONLY of the plan.

The ACTIVITY PLAN and FINANCIAL FORECASTS which form part of the total document need not be considered yet and are discussed later.

- Choose the headings you want to include in the business plan
- Decide what appendices you want and the detail to include
- Enter under each heading the points you wish to make, IN ONE OR TWO WORDS only, it in 'bullet point' form

This is so that, without unnecessary time and effort you can:

- Clear your ideas
- Decide what is important and what is not
- Alter and adjust
- Decide what does where

When you finished this draft move on to the next section.

THE ACTIVITY PLANS
INTRODUCTION

We have made the point that the business concept, however comprehensively defined, is little more than an aspiration and that what is subsequently needed is detailed planning TO TURN THE CONCEPT INTO REALITY.

Activity planning is all too often ignored in business plans and yet it is almost impossible to see how the business will hang together without going through the process at least at summary level, certainly in any but the very simplest of proposals.

Neither is it possible to prepare sound financial forecasts without going through the stage.

Preparation of the activity plans is a vital step and having completed an outline of the NARRATIVE PLAN (in bullet point form) you should now prepare a first draft of the activity plans.

Again, we use the term 'draft' because there will be a stage later when you will check that the outlines of the narrative section, the activity plans and the financial forecasts all say the same thing but in their own way!

GROUPING ACTIVITIES

You have already done half the task by listing in groups all the points that have come to mind – all you know have to do is put them in some sensible order.

If what follows seems a 'bit of a mouthful' refer to appendix E where we provide another example. Its not as difficult as it sounds when reading it!

PREPARE BLANK SHEETS AS FOLLOWS: TIME AT THE TOP MAY BE IN DAYS, WEEKS OR MONTHS WHICHEVER IS APPROPRIATE TO THE ACTIVITY.

GROUP									(Time may be days, weeks, months)	
ACTIVITY	1	2	3	4	5	6	7	8	⇒	⇒

(continue)

- For each group, one at a time, consider the points you have noted and

- Decide which are the major activities

- Order them according to which you think has to be done first, second, third and so on. In doing so, decide for each activity on two points:

- Which activity can and cannot be done before something else is done

- How long it will take to do the activity

- Describe the activity on the form and enter an 'a' in the boxes that cover the period of the activity

This is an iterative process as you will not get it right first time!

- Enter the key activities for each group first, without worrying about the more detailed level two and lower activities

- Review these 'level one' group sheets and prepare an overall activity chart from the group sheets

- Now with the two earlier points in mind decide:

- What can and cannot be done before something else is done

- How long it will take to do the task

'Juggle' the items on the summary and the group 'level one' charts until you are happy that you have the key activities in the right order and timing and that the 'whole fits together' at these two levels – summary and group level one.

. . . and a tip - *be conservative in your timing* - everything takes longer to organise and complete than you think - many matters are outside of your control . . .

- People go on holiday or fall ill – including you

- The printer will not get the colour right

- A piece of machinery arrives late

Since you will be relating your financial forecasts to the actitivity plan you will automatically build in this safety margin into your funding requirements.

When you have completed the summary and 'level ones' work through the next level of detail in each group:

- For each level one plan prepare a second level activity plan, again considering the two points made earlier

It is not usually necessary at this stage to go any lower in the levels of detail (unless you want to) and once you are happy that the skeleton hangs together, that is, that all the activities down to level two relate sensibly to each other, you can put the draft activity plans to one side.

FINANCIAL FORECASTING

INTRODUCTION TO FORECASTING

The third part of exercise is financial forecasting and for many readers this will be a daunting, even difficult exercise. Indeed, financial matters generally are one of the areas on which those starting in business are always advised to seek assistance.

We give later in FURTHER CONSIDERATIONS many of the matters that you and your advisors will have to think through in some detail at a later stage.

It is important that the financial forecast goes hand-in-hand with the narrative business plan and activity planning and we will come back to this point later.

The purposes of a financial forecast are as follows:

- To assess the financial viability of the business
- Is it going to make a profit and when?
- To ascertain the cash flows and how much funding is required. The likelihood is that business expenditure is going to be greater than the business income for a while. This shortfall in funding has to come from:

    Yourself

    Partners

    External Investors

    Other Lenders such as a bank

- To provide potential lenders with sufficient understanding of the business' finances to assess the risks involved – it is after all, the financial results that determine the viability of the proposal and whether or not the providers of funds are likely to have their money repaid.

Lenders will want evidence that all aspects of the business have been properly thought through.

The more you can demonstrate that the plans have been thought through, and

- The more the lenders can see how you are going to make the business work,
- The greater will be their confidence in YOU (and your management team), and that their investment will be repaid with a reasonable profit, and . . .
- The more likely they will be to advance the required funds

It will often be necessary to prepare two cash forecasts:

- The proposed BUSINESS flows, after showing the amount the business can afford to pay the owner(s) by way of salary
- Your PERSONAL flows:-
    To determine how much you can afford to invest to cover funding requirements
    To see how much you have cut back on personal expenditure until the business is off the ground.

If and when you have to prepare such a statement you should divide your income and expenditure into the following categories. You will then be able to determine your various levels of 'survivability':

- Certain Income
- Uncertain income
- Essential expenditure
- Important expenditure
- Desirable, but non-essential expenditure

See appendix G for more personal forecasting.

✱ ✱ ✱ ✱ ✱ ✱ ✱ ✱

REQUIREMENTS

What, then, is required? Again, except in the very simplest of businesses – our friendly window cleaner, for example – the requirements will include forecasts of:

- Profits and losses
- Balance Sheets
- Cash Flows
- The assumptions upon which the above is based
- Supporting analysis and calculations

Although dependent upon the use and complexity of the plan the information provided is normally required by:

- Month for the first twelve months, possibly longer, with totals for each quarter
- By quarter for the next two years
- By year thereafter

Just like activity planning, financial forecast is an interactive process – as you adjust your assessment of the market the sales figures will change. This, in turn, will change costs related to those sales, e.g. the direct costs of those sales, with knock-on effect to the cash flows (and profit and loss and balance sheets). The revised results must then be reviewed and other changes made if necessary – and so it goes on.

It will assist you enormously if you have access to even the simplest of computer spreadsheets to do the basic sums for you; it will also greatly assist in answering the inevitable 'what happens if . . . 'questions, for example, if you change the rate of build up of sales.

As we have said you may require assistance in preparing certain financial statements. This is principally because turning cash flows into profit and loss statements and balance sheets requires some understanding of accounting, for example, how to deal with:

- Credit taken and given
- Buildings, plants and equipment and their depreciation
- Leases
- Stocks and work-in-progress
- Standard methods of presentation

But a cash flow forecast – which many businessmen, in any case, regard as the most important document – is not that difficult to prepare and can be built up as information comes to hand.

Appendix H is a simple example; but bear in mind that a complicated case is exactly the same in principle, just more lines and greater sub-analysis!

For those who are financially minded we also provide the profit and loss account and balance sheet related to the example together with the accounting entries and some notes of explanation.

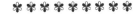

PRODUCT PRICING

Before I move to cash forecasting, however, we must consider product pricing, a key point to selling the product and ultimate business profitability.

There are really only 'two-and-a-half' questions to answer:

- What will customers pay for the product bearing in mind their needs, influences on demand, and so on?
- Will that price sustain a profitable business?

And two secondary questions:

- At what level of output?
- And by when?

The first question will be answered by research into the market – competition, demand, needs and so on.

The second question will be answered by building up your costs carefully.

And at the end of the day business financial viability is ONLY BASED on the above questions summarised as:

WHAT WILL THE MARKET PAY, HOW OFTEN, AND WHEN?

From what the MARKET will pay – CASH

- The direct costs of the product
- The indirect costs of the business
- The salaries of the owners
- Dividends to the investors
- Repayments and interest to the lenders
- Tax to the government

And keep something for a 'rainy day' and expansion.

In the following example we have established that the likely selling value per unit is £100.

We have estimated that the unit costs are built up as follows:

	£
Parts	-15
Owners Labour	-25
Packing	-5
Total	-45
Sales value	100
Contribution to overheads	55

We estimate what the total overheads for the year are to be and divide it by the number of units we hope to sell; the answer is £30 of overheads per unit.

Thus the net profit is £55 less £30, that is, £25; we have quickly ascertained that the price to the customer should bear the cost of the business and leave a profit.

Although we are going to concentrate in this section on cash forecasting, in this example we show the Profit and Loss Account; a P & L Account matches costs to incomes and in this case is as follows:

Month	1	2	3	4
Unit Sales value - £100				
Sales volume	10	20	30	50
Total unit volume for the year is 500				
	£	£	£	£
Total Sales value	1000	2000	3000	5000
Direct Costs	–450	–900	–1350	–2250
Gross Margin	550	1100	1650	2750
Overheads	–300	–600	–900	–1500
Net profit	250	500	750	1250

We will come back to how this is presented in cash forecast format.

INTRODUCTION TO CASH FORECASTING

When talking about profits and losses we use the terms income and expenditure but with cash forecast the words are RECEIPTS and PAYMENTS.

A Cash forecast simply shows:

- What amounts the business will RECEIVE and when
- What amounts the business will PAY and when
- The difference, the BALANCE

It can show as much or as little analysis as wanted.

PREPARING A CASH FORECAST

- You should enter the amounts you expect to PAY AND RECEIVE IN THE ACTUAL MOUTH YOU EXPECT TO MAKE THE PAYMENT OR RECEIVE THE INCOME
- You should ignore all taxes at this stage
- VAT should be ignored but if and when it becomes a factor it will affect cash flows
- Salaries and wages should be entered as gross payments – in practice, PAYE, NI and employees' pension will be paid to the government or a pension fund, and the net amount 'after deductions' to the employee, but it is unnecessary work at this stage to apportion between the recipients (unless you wish to)

- You should keep capital and revenue items separately

  Capital items are generally those which are tangible and will last the business for some time – plant, equipment, furniture, vehicles

  Revenue items are trading transactions representing the running of the business – receipts in respect of sales, payments in respect of purchases and expenses

- Revenue expenditure is usually divided into:

  Direct cost of sales – costs incurred in making the product

  Overheads – all other costs

- **The format below is split into a number of sections if you wish, you may build these up separately and transfer the total line only onto the summary – as we have done in appendix H**

Finally, like activity planning, what follows looks a lot more difficult than it really is; it is no more difficult than the cash forecasting you probably do for your own personal purposes.

FORMAT OF THE CASH FORECAST

A – The forecast should be named:

Name...

B – The forecast should be for a period:

CASH FLOW FORECAST FOR THE PERIOD

FROM (month & year)   TO (month & year)

C – The suggested columns are:

	1 J	2 F	3 M	Total 1-3	4 A	5 M	6 J	Total 1 - 6	→ →
Description	£	£	£	£	£	£	£	£	→

There should be an annual total after the fourth quarter total.

D – The suggested order of descriptive headings:

Presenting the receipts and payments in the following format will assist your financial advisors and bankers in assessing the best way to fund any shortfall.

Funding will be needed to keep any month end shortfall balance within agreed limits and how it is to be funded will depend on a number of considerations, outlined in FURTHER CONSIDERATIONS. Possibilities include:

- Allowed level of overdraft
- Injection of funds by the owners
  Up front
  As and when needed
- Bank loan repaid to a timetable
- Leasing plant and equipment

After considering the funding requirements the forecast will have to be adjusted for any interest costs and repayment scheme.

The format is as follows:

Trading Receipts	£
less	A
Trading Payments, cost of sales	B
Gross trading cash position	C=A minus B

This first level presents the gross cash surplus before you have paid for the businesses other revenue costs – overheads

less	A
Trading Payments, overheads	D
Gross trading cash position	E=C minus D

less	
Salary to the owner	F
Gross trading cash position	G=E minus F

E – Indicates whether or not the business can trade at a surplus before any payment to the owner, that is what is notionally available to him before all taxes; G is after the payment

less	
Capital Costs	H
The business cost	I=G minus H

I – The cash flow before the start-up costs

less	
Start-up payments	
Capital	J
Revenue	
The full financial cash flow	
position in the month	K=I minus J

K – is the net cash inflow or outflow the month and is carried down to the balance calculation

If any total is already a minus figure you must ADD the next line of expenditure.

Balance calculation	
Balance at the beginning	
of the month	L
Plus or minus the full financial	
cash flow	
Position in the month - K above	K
Balance at month end, c/f	M
Required funding	

✱ ✱ ✱ ✱ ✱ ✱ ✱ ✱ ✱

RECEIPTS AND FUNDING

I now provide a number of examples and payments you should consider but:

- It is not an exhaustive list – you can add and delete as necessary

- You can include items in groupings other than those we have shown

- You can create your own groupings

RECEIPTS AND PAYMENTS

A – Trading Receipts

- Sales trading – exclude VAT

B – Trading payments, cost of sales

- Purchases:
  Subcontractor Costs
  Materials
  Parts
  Packing
  Suppliers' delivery costs
- Salaries / wages – for making product
- Testing
- Delivery charges

C – Trading payments, overheads

- Premises
  Rent / lease – not if freehold
  Heat, light power
  Water
  Business Rates
  Insurance
  Security
  Cleaning
- Repairs and maintenance
  Premises
  Plant and equipment
  Vehicles
  Office equipment
  Computers
- Vehicles
  Insurance
  MOT
  Tyres
  Road fund tax
  Fuel
- Computers
  Rental
  Software
  Stationery
  Discs
- Staffing

Salaries and wages – enter gross
Employer pension Contribution
Employer NI Contribution
- Marketing
Advertising
Papers & Magazines
Promotional Leaflets
Postage
Envelopes
Entertaining
Travel
Exhibitions
- Communications equipment rentals
Fax
Answer phone
0800 number
- Other equipment rentals
Photocopier
Security Systems
- General
Travel
Insurance
Contents
Fire, theft
Employers liability
Consequential profits
Stationery
Letterhead
Calling cards
Envelopes
Financial
Incidentals
Coffee/tea
Postage
Telephone Charges
Fax
Answer phone
0800 number
Photo-copying
Paper
Registration fees
Data Protection
Associations
Bank Costs
Charges
Interest
Accounting and audit
Legal

- Other income
Bank interest
Grants

F – Salary to owner

This should be the GROSS amount that, after deductions for tax, after deductions for tax, pension (to a private scheme) and national insurance, leaves you with what you need to live on – the forecast of your personal position will determine what this figure should be.

H – Capital Costs

Capital items are those that will last for some period if time and are NOT part of your TRADING receipts and payments, those to do with making and selling your product.

Lease costs are treated in different accounting ways depending upon the nature of the lease and can in some cases be treated as if they were capital assets – advice will be needed. For the time being assume that lease costs are trading payments and include in C above.

If capital costs is needed at the beginning to get the business of the ground the costs should be included below in J – START UP COSTS.

Include payments in respect of the purchase of premises and capital equipment etc:

- Premises
Additions and extensions
- Plant and equipment
- Vehicles
- Computers and Printers
- Office equipment
Desks
Cabinets
Chairs
Photo-copier
Safe
FAX

Answer phone

Cupboards

J – Start up payments

These are payments you will have to make to get the business started; SUBSEQUENT replacements, restocking and renewals should be included in TRADING PAYMENTS OR CAPITAL COSTS.

- Capital payments

  Purchase price of:

  Business – if you buy a business

  Purchased premises

  Production plant and equipment

  Storage

  Transport

  Office equipment

  Computer/printer

- Revenue payments

  Legal fees

  Accountants fees

  Company registration – if trading as a limited company

  Alterations and additions

  Survey Costs – can be treated as capital payments in some cases

  Permissions

  Compliance with:

  Building and other regulations – can be treated as capital payments in some cases

  Fire

  Factory Acts

  Health & Safety

  Staff needs

  General security – can be treated as capital payments in some cases

  Decoration

  Initial insurance Premiums

  Advertising

  Stocks

Parts

Raw material

Stocks

Parts

Raw material

Consumables

Packing

Stationery

Letterhead

Calling Cards

Envelopes

ASSUMPTIONS

You must include a simple narrative explanation of the key assumptions plus calculations upon which the figures have been arrived at. The assumptions are important because they will:

- Remind you in the future of how you arrived at the figures
- Subsequently help identify where you were right and wrong
- Give the external reader an understanding of the figures when reviewing the plan alone
- Act as a process of clarification as you write them

We suggested that you prepare sub-sections for the major groups of receipts and payments:

- Sales
- Cost of sales
- Overheads
- Capital
- Start up costs

And we recommend that you prepare your assumptions under the same headings.

CASH FORECAST EXAMPLE

Finally, we said we would return to the presentation of the pricing model we gave earlier to show it in cash flow format. The unit direct costs were as follows:

	£
Parts	15
Owner's labour	25
Packing	5
Total	45

Overheads were estimated to be £30 per unit, and the selling price, £100 per unit.

Thus, to recap, the key figures were:

Month	1	2	3	4
	£	£	£	£
Total Sales Value	1000	2000	3000	5000
Direct costs	−450	−900	−1350	−2250
Overheads	−300	−600	−900	−1500
Net profit	250	500	750	1250

The calculation was done to see if the market price, a unit sales value of £100, would sustain the business – it was, in other words, a shorthand calculation – and it showed that the value produced a unit profit of £25.

The table then MATCHED THE COSTS OF THE SALES WITH THE SALES and showed the forecast results, the net profits, for the first four months of the business.

BUT this will not be how the cash flows look – assume only that:

- Sales receipts are received in the month
- It has been more economical to pay for four months stocks of parts and packing up front
- The labour for the four months is paid in equal amounts
- Half the overheads have to be paid three months in advance, for example rent, and the balance of overheads in the month

Month	1	2	3	4	Total
	£	£	£	£	£
Sales receipts	1000	2000	3000	5000	
Parts and packing for 110 units	−2200	-	-	-	
Labour -687	−688	−687	−688		
Gross cash flow	−1887	1312	2313	4312	
Overheads	−2500	−625	−625	--2500	
NET CASH FLOW	−4387	687	1688	1812	−200
ORIGINAL NET PROFIT	250	500	750	1250	2750

The overheads are calculated as follows:

a) 500 units in the year at £30 per unit totals £1500

b) Which is £3750 per year

c) Of which half is paid in advance, £1875

d) And the balance (£1875) equally each month, £625]

The results are quite different! and this is why it is almost more important to work in cash than profit. Although both will, as you can later prove, produce the same result for the year initial funding problems would not have been identified working in profit and loss format only.

You cannot, however, get away from presenting information in the profit and loss presentation because:

- All statutory accounting requires it (I.e. for a limited company)
- Tax is based on it

✳ ✳ ✳ ✳ ✳ ✳ ✳ ✳

WHAT HAS HAPPENED?

The DIRECT UNIT COSTS in the pricing model were apportioned in accordance with when the SALES of units were made RATHER THAN WHEN THE CASH WAS SPENT. In the second, cash is shown WHEN RECEIVED AND PAID.

Cash forecasting places receipts and payments in the month IN WHICH THEY WILL BE RECEIVED AND PAID AND DOES NOT TRY TO MATCH COSTS TO SALES – EXPENDITURE TO INCOME.

In our example the total of the monthly cash flows will be the same as the total of the monthly profits FOR THE YEAR AS A WHOLE because all of the timing differences will have worked themselves through.

To prove the point do both the profit and

cash flows for the remainder of the year based upon the same assumptions but using your own build up of unit sales, to a total of 500 for the year. Both results will come in total to:

500 units

	£
Sales of £100	50000
Direct costs of £45	−22500
	27500
Overheads of £30	−15000
Profit of £25	−12500

✳ ✳ ✳ ✳ ✳ ✳ ✳ ✳

THAT'S ALL THERE IS TO IT!

✳ ✳ ✳ ✳ ✳ ✳ ✳ ✳

WHAT SHOULD WE DO NOW?

Complete the cash forecast at least by:

- Month for the first twelve months, possibly longer, with totals for each quarter

And possibly longer

- By quarter for the next two years
- By year thereafter

Until business financial viability is demonstrated

- Prepare separate sub-sections for each main group of costs transferring only the total to the suggested format in D – Format of cash forecast given earlier.
- Prepare the RECEIPTS FORECAST FIRST, which should be analyzed in as much depth as possible. All other sub-forecasts depend on getting this one as right as possible. Preparing the analysis will make you think of the business from different points of view.

- Forecast the total number of product units you will sell.
- Analyze your sales by:
  Product line
  Major customer
  Geographic Area
- Sales build up through time
  Remember that business may be subject to peaks and troughs
  Seasons
  Holidays
- Remember that the totals for each analysis must be the same
- Evaluate the units sold by selling value, excluding VAT
- BE CONSERVATIVE
  Assume that your sales will build more slowly than you expect
- Once you are happy with the receipts forecast prepare PAYMENTS' forecasts for:
- Cost of sales
  By product line
- Overheads
- Capital
- Start up costs
- BE CONSERVATIVE
  Remember that the costs build faster than you expect
- If possible prepare your financial analysis on a spreadsheet. Once the format has been set up it will save much time and allow you to do the important 'what happens if...' analysis
- Some of the questions you will want answers to are 'what happens if':
- Sales
  Do not start as early as forecast?
  Start sooner than forecast?
  Build up more slowly/faster?

- The Market price is:
  Too high?
  Too low?
- Discounts are provided at different rates?
- A major customer is lost, or more than one?
- The selling mix of products is changed – more of A and less of B etc? &
- What is the lowest level of sales needed to support your salary?

You will have to asses each sub-forecast of costs in the light of the different receipts forecasts you prepare; through this iterative process you should arrive at four different financial views:

- The most optimistic
- The most pessimistic
- The forecast that sustains your minimum level of personal requirements
- The most realistic view of the future and the one which you will relate to the NARRATIVE and ACTIVITY PLANS

REMEMBER that if you adjust one assumption it will likely affect others. Suppose, for example, that you subsequently forecast that sales can be built up more quickly than currently shown this will probably mean that:

- Your payments for direct costs such as parts and materials has to increase
- Advertising activity and costs may have to be brought forward
- Wages may have to increase because you have to employ a salesman sooner than originally anticipated, production labour is increased earlier.

BUSINESS PLAN REVIEW

Your have now prepared the following:

- A draft NARRATIVE PLAN in bullet point form
- Draft ACTIVITY PLANS to level two
- At least a draft CASH FLOW FORECAST

Now is the time to put a 'cold towel round the head' and review the three documents together.

ALL THREE MUST BE IN HARMONY:

- THE TIMING OF CASH FLOWS MUST RELATE TO THE TIMINGS IN THE ACTIVITY PLANS
- THE ACTIVITY PLANS AND CASH FLOWS MUST AGREE IN THEIR OWN FORM TO THE BULLET POINT NARRATIVE PLAN

WHAT SHOULD WE DO NOW??

REVIEW THE CASH FLOWS FIRST TO SEE THAT:

- Sales receipts are correctly stated
- All costs are included, starting and ending in the appropriate month
- What can be done, THAT YOU CAN SUBSTANTIATE, has been done to improve the 'bottom line' by:
  reducing costs
  Increasing receipts
  Bringing forward receipts
  Delaying payments

This must be done HONESTLY AND FAIRLY. YOU MUST BELIEVE THAT THE FINANCIAL RESULTS ARE ATTAINABLE.

NOW REVIEW THE FINANCIAL FORECAST WITH THE ACTIVITY PLANS:

- To ensure that the underlying activities are correctly presented. For example, if you have changed the sales your recruiting and advertising activities may have to change as well.

FINALLY, BRING THE NARRATIVE PLAN IN LINE WITH THE FINANCIAL AND ACTIVITY PLANS – STILL IN BULLET POINT FORM.

CONTINUE JUGGLING THE THREE PARTS UNTIL YOU ARE HAPPY THEY ALL TELL THE SAME STORY IN THEIR OWN WAY.

ONLY WHEN YOU ARE HAPPY 'YOU ARE THERE' SHOULD YOU PREPARE THE SUMMARY TO THE BUSINESS PLAN – AGAIN BULLET FORM/

NOW STAND BACK
'IS THERE A BUSINESS?'

THIS IS THE ACID TEST. IS THE BUSINESS CASE:

- SOUND?
- CREDIBLE?
- ACHIEVABLE?

FINAL CHECK

Now flesh out the business plan in narrative style.

Remember that the plan will likely be read by others = you understand what you mean = will they?

- Use short words wherever possible
- Use short sentences rather than long ones
- Read each paragraph and ensure it says what you want it to say and that it flows In easy reading style
- Read each section and see that it flows in easy reading style
- Read the whole document to ensure it meets its purposes

THE NEXT STEPS

You now have a business plan that represents 'your best shot' and you have a choice to make:

- To seek professional advice
- To continue to 'go it alone'

If you are commercially and financially orientated and take an internet in accounting, tax and legal matters and have the time to learn by following your nose through the books, pamphlets and advice there is nothing to stop you continuing by yourself.

However, by far the more usual course of action, and the one that advisors on small business affairs invariably advocate, is to seek assistance through the next stages. We will come back to this option in a minute.

❉ ❉ ❉ ❉ ❉ ❉ ❉ ❉ ❉

If you want to 'go it alone' consider the points we make in FURTHER CONSIDERATIONS.

How formal you wish to make the final business plan is much dependent upon who is to read it and to what purpose it is to be used. However, we believe that after all the effort you have put into the exercise you deserve to have a nicely bound document.

We would certainly recommend that if it is to be read by a potential lender or investor that:

- It is TYPED – this really is a 'must' – it shows:

  Good image

  Serious intent

  A business-like approach
- It is CHECKED very carefully:

  Check all references

  Check that all financial tables add correctly

  Check that all calculations are correct

  Check that figures taken from a table agree to it

  Check that wording is concise
- SOMEONE ELSE READS and checks it – if they raise questions:

  Is your text clear?

  Is further work needed?

  Should further explanation be included?
- You DISCUSS it
- You REVISE and do a final check
- Perhaps you discuss it again
- You BIND it in a suitable cover

If you are going the 'advisor' route,, you will need to choose one, probably a specialist, who is familiar with business start-up work.

Personal recommendation is the best link to advice but you can also approach the local Chamber of Commerce or the local district society of the Charted Accountants in England and Wales for the names of practitioners who are experienced in such matters.

Consider a firm with between three and six partners – this size indicates an established practice but not big, used to dealing with small clients but large enough to have experienced services.

Most important of all choose someone YOU CAN GET ON WITH – he/she will be your financial friend and advisor for perhaps many years to come. Mutual trust is most important.

Once chosen he (or she!) will review your plan and take it from there . . . .

CONCLUSION

If you have followed my exercise diligently you will have prepared a very good business plan, and with good advisors you will have taken all the practical steps needed to set up on the road to success.

If it seems to have a lot of effort, perhaps a little 'over the top' at times remember:

Our experience tells us, time and time again, that the more work that goes into a busiiness before its launch the better it will work afterwards.

VERY GOOD LUCK!

❀ ❀ ❀ ❀ ❀ ❀ ❀ ❀ ❀

PART D - FURTHER CONSIDERATIONS

FURTHER CONSIDERATIONS - UK

This section includes any of the other matters that will have to be considered in setting up in business. You will find that they often overlap with points we have already raised and with themselves because most, if not all, issues in business are inter-related in some way or another – usually money!

Many of the points refer to statutory and tax issues which easily become out of date. We have tried to ensure that the information is correct but you will understand that matters do change.

And beware . . . . !

A little knowledge is a dangerous thing!

Treat the points as mind-joggers – each one invariably leads on to many other related points.

1. ACCOUNTING

1.1 Transactions

- Most business decisions give rise to a money transaction
- Transactions to be recorded
- Original documents wherever possible must be retained to evidence the transaction
  Sales and purchase invoices
  Expense vouchers
  Bank statements
  Agreements
  Leases
  Title document

1.2 Records – most business will need the following to record transactions

- Cash book
- Petty Cash book
- Purchase day book
  Analysis
- Purchase Leger
  Records who you owe money to
- Sales day book
  Analysis of your sales
- Sales ledger
  Records who owes you money
- General Ledger
  Records all other transactions including
  Expenses
  Wages and salaries
  Fixed assets
  Sometimes these transactions are recorded in separate ledgers

1.3 Information

- Cash and bank
  Receipts
  Payments
  Balance
- Sales
  Analysis of sales by product
  Amounts owed by debtors
  Invoicing customers
  Statements sent to customers
  Debt collection
- Expenses
  Invoices and receipts
  Analysis by type
- Stock
  Type
  Raw materials
  Parts

Finished goods

Work-in-progress

Balance of items in stock

Amount

Cost

Value

- Fixed assets

Nature

Buildings

Equipment

Fittings & fixtures

Vehicles

Cost

Depreciation

Value

- Funding paid in

Nature

1.4 Auditing

- No statutory requirement except in the case of limited companies

Law changing on requirement for an audit

- Other government agencies have right of access to audit certain records

Customs and Excise

Inland Revenue

PAYE

Business Tax

2 BANKING

2.1 General Points

- Shop around to find the best arrangements for you
- Keep business banking separate from personal banking
- Keep bank account and reconciliation up to date
- Bank cheques and cash at earliest possible time

2.2 Costs

- Know what it costs to keep the account

Transactions charges

Interest earned and paid

Serious penalties for exceeding agreed borrowing limits

Postage of cheque / bank transfer

2.3 Methods of payment

- Cheque
- Cash
- Standing Order
- Direct Debit
- Bankers order
- Bankers Draft

3 BUSINESS TAX FOR INDIVIDUALS AND PARTNERSHIPS

3.1 General

- Must tell Tax Office when you start in business

Customs & Revenue

- f you employ someone you will have to account for the PAYE and NI due

3.2 Assessments

- The tax year runs from 6th April in one year to the 5th April in the following year
- Tax levied on taxable profits not turnover
- The assessment relates to a tax year
- The assessment for one tax year is on the trading profits of your trading year ended in the previous tax year

Accounting year is 12 months to 31st;March; the tax you pay in the tax year 2010/11 is based upon the profits for your accounting year to 31st March 2009

- There are special rules for the first and last years of a business

- If Tax Office not happy with your return of income it may raise an estimated assessment of profits

3.3 Losses

- The first 4 year's losses can be set against the income of the previous three years' income of whatever sort
  Perhaps even before you started trading, e.g. if were employed
  Claim to be made within 2 years from tax year in which loss is made
- For any year, not just the first 4, you can have any loss set against other income of that tax year
- A loss may be carried forward to be set against future profits

3.4 Return of income

- Required by law to make a return of income each year
- Return includes business profits
- You should send your business accounts with the return or
  before the return if your accounting date is before the return is due
- The return is YOUR RESPONSIBILITY even if you retain an accountant to prepare it for you

3.5 Appeal

- If you disagree with your assessment you may appeal within 30 days
  may appeal later than 30 days in some instances
- You may appeal against the amount of tax you are being asked to pay

3.6 Expenditure

- To be allowable for tax purposes the expenditure must be wholly and exclusively for the business
- Expenditure that is both private and business may be split between the two

- Expenditure before business commenced may be allowable
  If incurred up to 5 years before business started
  If the expenditure would have been allowable if the business had already started
  BUT stock and items qualifying for capital allowances are treated as allowable from the first day of trading
- Accounting depreciation is not allowed per se but capital allowances are given in place of

3.7 General Accounting

- Business must keep accounting records
- Full accounts i.e., profit and loss and balance sheet are not required if business takings before expenses are below £30000
- The accounting date of your business, the date to which your annual accounts are made up, is important and you should seek advice

3.8 Additional rules related to partnerships

- One assessment made on the partnership profits
- Because all parents are liable for all debts of the partnership each partner is liable for all the tax liability
- Special rules apply when a partner starts or leaves the business

3.9 Calculating taxable profits

- Complicated and extensive rules
- In general
  Capital expenditure is not allowable
  But capital allowances are
  Revenue expenses are allowable.

BUT . . .

4 BUYING A BUSINESS
4.1 General
- Retain a solicitor or accountant to negotiate the purchase contract
- All negotiations must be confidential and subject to contract
- Vendor must be asked to provide assurances in the purchase contract regarding the state of the business
- Strike a relationship if possible with the vendor in order to get to know as much as possible about:

  Customers

  Accounting

  Employees

  Suppliers

  Facilities
- Arrange for finance and funding before purchase
- Finding a business

  'Marriage bureaus' agencies

  Determine what fees are payable, if any

  Newspapers

  Trade magazines

  Specialist 'businesses for sale' magazines

4.2 Financial and general business position to be looked at in detail by an accountant
- Last three years' accounts
- Management information
- Contingent liabilities

  Outstanding litigation
- Value of assets

  Value of stocks and work-in-progress

  Age / Use
- Tax position
- Order Book
- Good will if business makes a loss or poor results?

4.3 What is being sold / purchased?
- Share capital – the whole business
- Cash, liabilities and debts to be
- Business assets – premises, plant and equipment, vehicles and stocks – goodwill

4.4 Valuation
- Considerable taxation questions

  VAT may be a consideration

  Beware tax loses

  Will they be useable by new business?
- Limited company may be valued according to

  New assets and/or

  Potential earnings

  Profits to be calculated after a reasonable salary to the new owner

5 EMPLOYMENT
5.1 General
- Keep good records up to date
- Data Protection Act may apply
- Records are audited – PAYE
- Details

  When started

  Promotion

  Changes in pay or other terms and conditions

  Disciplinary and grievance matters
- Should provide evidence against any action brought for discrimination or harassment

5.2 Recruitment
- Job Description

  Required qualities

  Responsibilities

  Education

  Expertise

  Age

  Experience

  Package and benefits

- Remember lead time in recruitment including period of notice of potential employee
- Recruitment of good people takes time

5.3 Employment
- Different rights depending on time worked per week and length of employment
- Terms and conditions to be provided for all employees

  Details of pay and calculation, intervals and hours of work, holiday pay

  Holiday entitlement

  Sick pay

  Pension arrangements

  Notice period

  Disciplinary rules and grievance problems
- Dismissal

  Reasons to be given after 6 months employment

  Unfair rules apply after 1 years of employment
- Period of Notice

  1 week after a month

  A week a year up to 12 years (i.e. 12 weeks notice)

  Notice can be lengthened but not shortened less than statutory minimum
- Handling redundancies

  Redundancy pay after 1 year if over 18 years
- Employee's rights if business goes into liquidation
- Rights if expectant mother
- Suspension on medical grounds
- Union membership rights
- Itemised payslips
- Rights on the transfer of a business

- Time off for public duties
- Sex and racial discrimination
- Equal Pay
- Disabled workers

5.4 Training
- Who
- When
- How

6 FINANCIAL REPORTING
6.1 General
- Statutory requirements for companies
- All organisations required to keep records to satisfy taxing authorities

6.2 Regular Financial Reporting
- Setting of financial budgets
- Weekly and monthly cash receipts and payments
- Quarterly profit and loss accounts
- Annual profit and loss account and balance sheet
- Government returns

  VAT

  PAYE / NI

  Possibly

  Company's annual return

  Company accounts

6.3 Management reporting
- Product Profitability
- Production

  Cost

  Scrap / waste

  Capacity and efficiency
- Stock levels
- Departmental budgets
- Employee attitudes
- Sales analysis

  Product

  Customer

- Customer Satisfaction

  Price

  Delivery

  Quality

  Delivery achievement against customer requirement
- Order book

  Product

  Customer

6.4 Budgeting and forecasting

- Budget usually set for a month, quarter and year and never changes
- Forecasts reassess the view for the budgeted period

Thus, the forecast for the year may be reassessed as the actual results become known:

	Actual To date £	For Year Budget £	Forecast £
Sale at end of:			
Month 3	4000	15000	16000
Month 6	9000	15000	19000
Month 9	14500	15000	20000

7 FORMING A COMPANY

7.1 General

- For simple and / or speedy situations buy a ready-formed one from an agent

  Cost £150 / £250

7.2 Essential Points

- Some care must be taken in agreeing the name
- Governing Documents are

  Memorandum and Articles of Association

  Set out what the company is formed for

  States what the company and its officers can and cannot do

Special considerations may be needed for directors and shareholder arrangement
- Certificate of Incorporation

  Company cannot trade until issued
- Company forming agents can normally check on possible infringement of patents and trademarks
- Company must have at least two shareholders
- Company must have at least one director
- Company must have secretary who cannot be the only director
- A Company mist hold a first meeting of directors to:

  Appoint additional or new directors

  Appoint secretary

  Appoint auditors

  Determine the financial year end

  Determine banking arrangements

  Make arrangements for keeping the statutory books

8 FUNDING – EQUITY CONSIDERATIONS

8.1 General

- Usually described as 'risk capital' since the investors have no guarantee of the return of their investment or any income on it
- Outside shareholders mean to the dominant shareholder:

  Possibly less control

  A smaller share of the company and what it is worth
- Special arrangements needed to value the shares of a private company – no ready market for the shares as a for a public company quoted on a Stock Exchange

8.2 Types of equity

- Many Types
  Ordinary with varying rights
  Preferred
  Redeemable and non-redeemable
  Cumulative and non-cumulative
  Transferable and non-transferable
- Memorandum of Association fives rights of shareholders

8.3 Ordinary Shares

- Ordinary shareholders own the company
- They control the company through voting arrangements
- Normally entitled to profits and capital growth in shares

8.4 Preferred Shares

- Carry the right to a share of profits (usually at a fixed rate) before any dividend to the ordinary shareholders
- Preferred shareholders receive their investment back before the ordinary shareholders in a winding up
- Preferred shareholders usually have no / limited voting rights
- If income not paid in one year the right to it may be carried forward to following years if the share is 'cumulative'
- Usually not so much appreciation in share value compared to ordinary shares

9 FUNDING – GENERAL ISSUES
9.1 General

- Always approach three or four bankers to get different views, comments on your business plan and financing ideas
  Amend plan in the light of comments

- Understand your business before you start to explain to bankers
- Gearing
  High when debt is large in relation to equity
  High interest cost

9.2 Ways to fund a business

- Internal
  Using reserves, using working capital more efficiently
- Debt financing, borrowing
  Fees to arrange
  Interest cost
- Share Capitals
- Other
  Leasing of assets
  Factoring debts (selling them)
  Government grants

9.3 Requirement defines type

- Match type of funding to needs
  Short-term needs with short-term debt
  Long-term needs with long-term debt
- Short term for working capital
  Usually overdrafts
  Simple and fast to arrange
  Subject to periodic review
  Technically repayable on demand, but rarely
- Medium and long-term for core needs and fixed asset
  Leasing of assets
  Bank
  Formal with agreed repayment arrangement
  Up to 30 years
  Various repayment schemes
  Interest may be fixed or floating
  Problems
  Formal and fixed
  Fixed rate may be high

If business is good loan may not be needed

Equity for the risk

Usually from the owner

10 FUNDING – INTERNAL

10.1 Control of stock levels

- Age of stock
- Use of stock

10.2 Control of credit given to customers

- Impose credit limit
- Monitor position at least weekly
- Chase on time
- Negotiate payments in advance
- Invoice as early as possible

10.3 Factoring of debts

- Short-term finance for working in capital needs
- Selling of debts to a company for immediate cash
- Typically:

  80% of debt may be advanced at once

  20% less factor's charges will be paid when debit paid

  The factor runs the sales ledger with administrative consequences

- Depending on nature of customer and business factor may bear all bad debts, for increased charges – known as 'without recourse' factoring
- 'with recourse' means you bear bad debts
- Invoice discounting is similar to factoring

10.4 Negotiation of terms of payment to suppliers

- Possible if you are a large customer
- Consider value of discounts

11 FUNDING – LEASE UP

11.1 General

- Useful short and medium-term funding – up to 10 years
- Relatively short-life assets, equipment, vehicles
- Two key types with different accounting treatments
- Finance lease and HP where the lessee is fully responsible for repairs, maintenance and insurance as if he owned the asset – but he doesn't'
- Operating lease – in effect a rental agreement
- Easy and quick to arrange
- Tax treatment for HP and lease are different and should be considered
- Leased asset is never owned by the lessee; asset bought on HP becomes property of lessee at end of agreement
- Sale and lease back arrangement whereby owner buys an asset, sells it to a leasing company and leases it back
- Discuss these arrangements with advisors, bankers and finance houses

12 FUNDING – WHAT THE BANKER CONSIDERS

12.1 General

- The banker will need to be satisfied that money is being lent to reputable customers who are competent to successfully to run their business and who themselves have some capital at risk in the business

12.2 Special Considerations

- What are purpose, amount and timing of borrowing?
- What is proportion of borrowing to assets?
- What security is there?
  Loans may have to be secured against personal or partnership assets
  Consider hard
  Difficulty to borrow more
  Consult lawyer on personal mortgages or on business assets
  High Interest
- Long-term commitment to repay the facility
  Difficult to borrow more
  More difficult to sell mortgaged property?
- What is the repayment plan?
  What is ability to repay?
  How / When?
- What is risk to lender?
- Does management seem competent and credible?
- What management experience has it?
- Is the money really needed?
- Profits sufficient to bear the interest cost?
- Are there other borrowings
  What are the terms of the borrowing
  Have the terms of the advance been met?
  Any defaults?
- Is the owner putting money at risk himself?
- Have profits been built up in the business?

13 FUNDING – WHY START-UP'S FAIL TO ATTRACT FINANCE

13.1 General

- Weakness in management
- Poorly presented proposals
- Inadequate security
- Imbalance between personal and lenders risk
- Too ambitious
- Lack of repayment plan
- Inherent business weakness
- Too many risks in the venture

14 NAME AND STATIONERY

14.1 Name

- Companies are restricted in their choice of names
- 'business' name does not have to be the same as its legal name and registered address prominently outside each place of business
- You must not 'pass off' yourself or your business as someone else's – intentionally or otherwise
  Check the name of a limited company through the registrar of companies or your agent
- Name may be important to image

14.2 Stationery

- Do not have stationery printed until name is agreed
- Certain information must be included on different documents – letterheads, orders etc
- Letterheads must include:
  Business name
  Legal Name
  Registered address, number and where registered
  All or none of the directors' name

- Where a business name is used for a sole trader or partnership of less than 20 partners letterheads, orders, invoices etc must include

  The names of each partner or sole trader

  The business address at which a document may legally be served

- Special rules apply to partnerships of more than 20

15 LEGAL CONSTRAINTS
15.1 Legislation
- Companies Acts
- Partnership Act
- Data Protection Act
- Landlord and Tenant Act
- Factories, Shops & Premises Acts
- Health & Safety at Work Act
- Consumer Credit Act
- Consumer Protection Act
- Employment Act
- Trade Description Act
- Patents Act

15.2 Codes of practice apply
- Is your business one that has to be licensed?

16 NATIONAL INSURANCE
16.1 General
- 5 Classes

  1 – Employed Persons

  1a – By the employer on cars used for private use

  2 – Self employed persons

  3 – Voluntary Contributions

  4 – Earnings related payable by self-employed

16.2 Class 2 – Self employed persons
- Flat rate payable weekly, including holidays
- Sole traders and partners
- Over 16
- Under pension age
- Payable either monthly or quarterly in arrears
- Contributions do not entitle to unemployment benefit
- Excused payment if profits are below a set limit

16.3 Class 4 – Earnings related also payable by self-employed
- On profits above a certain level
- In addition to the class 2
- Only half of class 4 may be chargeable against income
- Paid with income tax to the inland revenue
- Special deferment rules if you are both employed and self-employed

17 NATURE OF BUSINESS ORGANISATION
17.1 Form of trading entity
- Usual types

  Limited Company

  Partnership

  Sole Trader
- Unusual Types

  Company limited by guarantee

  Unlimited Company

  Limited Partnership

  Co-operatives

17.2 Company

- Advantages

  Shareholders' debt limited to capital put in

  Creditors cannot pursue claims to shareholders unless personal guarantees have been given, e.g. to a banker, or a fraud involved

  Sometimes greater creditor confidence

  Image

  A Separate 'person' in law, from the shareholders

  The business can often be more easily sold

  Continues after the death of a shareholder(s)

  Tax advantages re pension rights can be secured

- Disadvantages

  Administrative burden

  Legal matters

  Accounting

  Government returns

  Some information is public

  Financial Position

  Mortgages

  Directors and shareholders

  Legal Burden

  Governed by company law – extensive and sometimes onerous

  Compliances

  Minutes of meetings

  Duties of directors and secretary

  Costs

  Accounting and auditing (rules on latter are changing)

  Incorporation

  Filing of annual report

  Tax and other financial advice

  National insurances charges higher than for partnership and sole trader

  Difficulty in making loans to directions

  Lenders usually want guarantees from directors – minimising of liability protection

  General

  Care to be taken in choosing name

  Directors to be chosen

  Share structure to be agreed

  Corporation tax applies

17.3 Partnership

- Advantages

  No legal incorporation

  In absence of other agreement, Partnership Agreement 1890 applies

  Better to have one agreed by the partners

  Affairs are private – no information need be made public

  Legal compliances are relatively few

  Less onerous legal compliances on partners than directors – other than unlimited liability

  National insurance charges are less than for an employee

- Disadvantages

  Partner have unlimited liability for the debts of the business, usually separately and together – you are responsible for all the debts of the whole partnership

  No 'legal entity' that can be sold or transferred (does not mean partnership cannot be sold)

  Management freedom may be limited

  State benefits are less than for an employee

- General

  Partnership is technically dissolved and recommenced on any change in the partners

  Two or more individuals can form a partnership

  Partners bound by personal agreement and / or Partnership Act

  Usual matters dealt with include

  Name of business

  When it starts

  What the business is

  Capital put in by partners

  Sharing of profits and losses

  Drawing rights – taking out of cash in advance of profits

  Change in partnership

  Introduction of a new partner

  Expulsion of partner

  A partner leaving

  Retirement and death of a partner

  Dissolving the partnership

  Dealing with assets and liabilities including goodwill on a change in partnership

  Responsibilities of partners

  Accounting and banking matters

  Holidays and sickness

  Voting rights

  Partnership disputes

- Special tax rules

  Based upon personal rather than corporation tax rules

17.4 Sole Trader

In general the same advantages and disadvantages accrue to a sole trader as do to a partnership.

Additionally:

- Advantages

  Completed management freedom

  Master of own destiny

  No delay in decision taking

  Takes all the profits (and losses)

  Limited specific legislation mainly to do with the trading name and address

  No formal procedures are needed to set up as a sole trader

  Affairs are private

- Disadvantages

  Works alone

  No one to share work burdens

  Sole trader provides all the capital and takes all the risks alone

  Takes on full business activity

  Who manages when on holiday or ill?

  Totally responsible for the business and its debts and liabilities

  The business is inseparable from the individual

  Business dies with the individual

  More difficult to sell

  Capital and funding for expansion may be restricted

  If a creditor starts proceedings for recovery you may have to pay all debts at once

18 ORGANISATION AND ADMINISTRATION

18.1 General staffing arrangements and welfare

18.2 Procedures

- Written
- Updating

18.3 Meetings

- Who
- When
- Minutes

18.4 Division of responsibilities

- Chart
- Written

18.5 Insurance

- Tax implications
- Discuss requirements with several brokers
- Need?

  Employer's liability

  Motor Vehicles

  Public liability

  Fire and special perils

  Consequential loss

  Employment protection

  Indemnity

  Fidelity guarantee

  Engineering

  Product Liability

  Goods-in-transit

  Work-in-progress

  Personal accident

  Theft and burglary

  Plate glass

  Sickness, health, pensions

18.6 Security

- General access
- Passes

19 PREMISES

19.1 Mobile Shop

19.2 Location needs

- Near?

  Water

  Rail

  Road

  Air Transport

  Easy supplier deliveries

  Easy customer deliveries

  Removal costs

  Hill or flat

  Subsidence

  Security

19.3 Manufacture, process, service

- Floor area
- Floor loading
- Height
- Stock

  Special storage

- Drainage
- Loading bays
- Expansion

  Planning permissions

  Change of use

- Light
- Ventilation
- Power, water, disposal

19.4 Staff

- Travel
- Canteen
- Parking
- Smoking / non-smoking

19.5 Customers

- Image important / unimportant
- Parking important / unimportant

19.6 Health & Safety

- Fire Precautions

  Escapes

- Lighting
- Ventilation

19.7 General Working Conditions

- Environment

  Noise

  Traffic

  Aircraft

  Neighbours

- Lighting
- Neighbours

  Compatibility

19.8 General
- Local development policies
- Grants
- Compliances with
  Health and Safety at work act
  Offices, shops and railways premises act
  Factories acts
  Specific regulations
- Tax matters
- Insurance Matters

19.9 Nature of Agreement
- Purchase
  Condition
  Survey
  Roof
  Drains
  Decoration
- Freehold
  Other costs and restrictive covenants
- More initial capital but
  Security available for future borrowings
  Growth in value
  Easier to sell than lease
- Planning permissions
  Change of use
- Lease
  Planning permissions
  Change of use
  Length
  No long-term liability if business not secure
  Other costs and restrictive covenants
  Who is responsible for
  Insurance?
  Repairs?
  Internal and external decorations?
  Assignment

Sub-Lease
Comparison of costs
Any premium?
Rent reviews
Uniform business rate
- Contracts review by solicitor and / or accountant

20 REGISTRATIONS
20.1 General
- Possibly VAT
- PAYE and NI
- Corporation VAT
- Health and Safety 1974
- Data Protection
  If you maintain personal details on computer

20.2 Specialised
- Some more usual ones
  Betting shop
  Local magistrate
  Café, Restaurant
  Environmental health dept.
  Caravan site
  Local authority
  Children's nursery
  Social services dept.
  Food manufactures
  Environmental health dept.
  Hairdressers
  Local authority
  Ice Cream
  Public health dept.
  Market Stalls
  Local Health authority
  Mobile food stores
  Environmental health dept.
  Nursing agencies & homes
  Social services dept.
  Pet shops and kennels
  Environmental health dept.
  Riding stables
  Local authority

21 VALUE ADDED TAX

21.1 General

- A tax on transactions related to the supply of most goods and services in the UK and Isle of man
- A tax on certain imported goods
- You become a taxable person and must REGISTER for VAT purposes if:
  You are in business and
  Intend or do make TAXABLE supplies
  And taxable TURNOVER, NOT PROFIT, exceeds or will exceed a certain level, currently £68,000 (2011)
- Taxable turnover is the value of taxable supplies
- You may choose to become a taxable person even if your turnover is below the set limit, if customs and excise allow
- Tax charged by you on your taxable supplies is called output tax
- Tax charged to you by your suppliers is your input tax

21.2 Returns

- Due periodically
  Deduct the **input tax charges to you from the output tax charged by you** and pay or receive the amount due to / from customs and excise

21.3 Tax rates change and are currently

- 20%, standard rate
- 0%, zero rate
  Zero rated goods are taxable supplies where the rate is 0% and include:
  Most food but not catering supplies
  Books and newspapers
  Sales, long leases and construction of new houses
  Young children's clothing and footwear
  Export of goods

21.4 Exempt goods are not taxable supplies and include:

- Most property sale. Letting and leases of land and buildings.
- Insurance
- Some aspects of betting, gaming and lotteries
- Provision of credit
- Certain education and training supplies
- Services of doctors, opticians and dentists
- Certain supplies of undertakers

21.5 Registration

- Simple from VAT 1
- Number issued

21.6 Other matters

- Records to be kept and right of inspection by Customs and Excise
- Penalties are heavy for abuse of system
- Questions to be considered in greater detail
  Who has to be registered for VAT?
  Voluntary Registration?
  VAT before registration?
  When to start charging VAT?

22 VIEW OF BUSINESS OBJECTIVES

- 'Entrepreneurial' where owner sees company as chance to build up wealth
- 'Proprietorial' where owner's objective may be to provide a living, wealth being a side issue
- What do you want out of the business?
- When do you want to get your money?
- Will you ever want to go public?
- Honestly consider your objectives for the business

FURTHER CONSIDERATIONS - EXPORTING

1. GENERAL MATTERS

1.1 Exporting requires specialist knowledge, consider:

- Language
- Travel

  Cost
- Disputes more difficult to resolve

  Legal problems

  Cost of litigation

  Distance
- Consideration amount of advice available

  ### SEEK AND TAKE IT

  Start with DTI

  Croner's Reference Book for Exports

1.2 Markets

- Spread of risks

  If UK is bad overseas may be good and vice versa
- Technical and quality standards to comply with
- Retain a good agent in each market
- Price

  F A S – Free alongside, price includes delivery to docks

  F O B – Free on board – price includes delivery on to the ship

1.3 Shipping

- Packing and shipping matters
- Import regulations

  Invoicing and import regulations must be met precisely
- If by sea or air

  Retain a member of the Institute of Freight Forwarders who can advise on

Best method of transportation

Freight calculations and documents

Insurance

Collect and pack goods if required

2   FINANCE FOR EXPORT

Export finance assists exporter between shipping goods and receiving overseas remittance.

2.1 Short -term finance

- Sterling or currency bank overdrafts
- Discounting or negotiating bills of exchange
- Factoring
- Bank advances

2.2 Longer term finance

- Specific loans
- Supplier credit
- Buyer credit
- Project finance
- Line of credit

2.3 Government's Export Credits Guarantee Department provides insurance protection

- Credit risk – where the buyer cannot or refuses to pay for the goods
- Transfer and political risk – where a change in exchange controls, government, war, etc. Prevents payment
- Banks may advance finance against an ECGD policy
- Is dependent upon the assessed risk of trading with a particular part of the word
- ECGD is an insurance policy and premiums are payable

2.4 Payment

- Cash
- Letter of credit

  Exporter receives payment from bank on presentation of a FULL AND COMPLETE set of documents

  Types

  Irrevocable confirmed – no recourse to you

  Unconfirmed irrevocable – changed only by agreement

  Revocable not secure
- Drafts

2.5 Remember

- That overseas trade takes much longer to settle
- That chasing debts will be more difficult
- To negotiate with you suppliers where possible better payments terms to help finance the delay
- That the cost of finance must be considered
- Currency exposure

Appendix A - Business Concept

Please note the nature of your business idea as clearly as possible

Appendix A1 - a second draft of your Business Concept

Be precise and stick to the bullet points we have provided
●
●
●
●
●
●
●
●
●
●
●
●
●
●
●
●
●
●
●
●
●

Appendix A2 - Final statement of your Business Concept

Be precise and stick to the bullet points we have provided
•
•
•
•
•
•
•
•
•
•
•
•
•
•
•
•
•
•
•
•

Appendix B - Brainstorming

-
-
-
-
-
-
-
-
-
-
-
-
-
-
-
-
-
-
-
-

APPENDIX C ~ MARKETING

The Most difficult part of the business plan is assessing sales (and then achieving them!) and this appendix is to assist you in your market research.

Marketing is not the same as selling, Marketing is the whole activity involved in determining customer needs and desires, product development to meet those needs, advertising and selling and delivering the product you already have.

- Product strategy and policy
- Market strategy and policy
- Pricing strategy
- Promotional strategy and policy
- Physical distribution strategy and policy

Strategy is long-term aims; policy is short-term actions and plans.

Assessment usually depends on market research and any other information and evidence that can be found and we now give some ideas on the subject.

1 DEMAND
1.1 Buyer Influences
- Rejection of the product
  Why
- Changes in needs
  What
  Why
  How
  When
- Freedom
  Choice of supplier
- Motives
- Why he wants to buy

1.2 Demand elastic or not
- How is demand affected by price?
  Is demand there regardless of price?
  Does demand vary with small changes in price?

2 MARKET DETERMINATION
2.1 Although we have raised some of the points already you will want to ascertain if possible:
- Total Market size now
- Total potential size of market
- How is market changing
  Why
- Factors affecting demand
- What are the customers' requirements
- How the customer measures satisfaction
- Trends in product demand
- Competitors' strengths and weaknesses
- Avenue of potential product development
- What alternatives the customer has in supply
  Also substitutes for the product

2.2 The following may be useful sources of information as well as places to advertise:
- Newspapers
- Local Advertising papers and magazines
  Industrial exchange and mart
- Trade Magazines
- Competitor sales literature
- Trade telephone directories
- Local radio
- TV

- Exhibitions
- Posters
- Placards
- Direct Mail
- Inserts in paper
- Advertising agencies
- Door-to-door leaflets and brochures
- Newspaper shop windows
- Supermarket Notice boards
- Display in your own vehicle
- Purchase of customer lists
- Cinemas
- Leaflets left on car windscreens

3 MARKETING PITFALLS

- Lack of knowledge of the market
- Competing on price rather than product uniqueness
- Pricing too low leaving insufficient margin for price competition and expansion
- Launching new products without adequate research
- Staying in declining markets
- Complacency when matters are going well

4 MARKETING RESEARCH

4.1 Consider

- Economic Research
  Economy of region etc
- Market Research
  Detailed review of the particular Market
  Prices
  Changes in market trends
  Factors affecting the market
- Demand studies
  What affects demand

- Consumer studies
  Why people buy
  Habits
  Behaviour
  Patterns
  When
- Competition research
  Who
  What they are doing
  Their Products
  Are they successful? – Why / why not?
- Product Research
  What is needed, when, why?
  Quality needed
- Sales Research
  True sales pattern
  Why it is what it is
- Distribution Research
  Best methods of
  Customers needs
  Better service than competition
- Promotional Research
  What are the best means of promotion
  Why
  Timing thereof
- Effectiveness of each aspect of the above research

5 PROMOTION

5.1 Advertising
- Media selection
- Size, type of advert, colour
- Frequency

5.2 Sales
- Special activities over a particular period

  Discounts

  Free offers

  Branded packs

  Coupons

  Displays

  Posters

  Free gifts

  Exhibitions, seminars, conferences

5.3 Public Relations
- Keeps public awareness
- Press and TV
- Dinners
- Open days

6 RESEARCH REFERENCES

What research has already been done? – A GOOD LIBRARY IS A PRIME SOURCE OF INFORMATION and one of the best are the:

STATISTICS AND MARKET INTELLIGENCE LIBRARY
DTI, VICTORIA STREET, LONDON

There are quite literally thousands of reference books, trade directories and organisations which provide an enormous amount of information on just about any subject you wish to research; here are just a few of the more general references (publisher in brackets) and you should also refer to out booklet REFER which has a wide range of general business references.

- Croner's Exporters Reference Book
- The research index – an index to articles of general financial interest in over 100 periodicals
- Key Note Reports – a comprehensive series of market assessments
- Mintel – Market Intelligence reports on a range of market areas
- Which? Consumer reports
- Census of Distribution – Sales and other data for the retail trade, and other trade statistics
- Specific trade references and organisations
- The local Chamber of Commerce directories
- The UK's 10000 Largest Companies (ELC International)
- Personal Managers Year Book – details of all consultants and agencies handling a very wide range of human resource issues
- Who's who
- The Civil Service Year Book – a complete guide to all government ministries, agencies and organisations including addresses, telephone numbers and appointments
- Directory of publishers
- Directory of directors
- The Marketing Handbook – all agencies covering all aspects of marketing activity
- Brad – similar to the above
- Individual counties' directories of companies
- Individual company's accounts
- Statistical analyses (Central Statistical Office)
- Economic Outlook (London Business School)
- Economic Trends (Central Statistical Office)
- Monthly Digest of Statistics (Central Statistical Office)

- Business Monitor
- Quarterly Survey of Small Businesses (Small business Research Trust)
- The Employment Gazette – a wide range of employment information
- Population Trends
- Business Information Review – information on information services (Headland press)
- CSO Bulletins (Central Statistical Office) – a range of commercial and personal statistics

- Conference and Exhibitions Fact Finder
- Kompass – a national directory of UK companies (Reed information Services Ltd)
- Key British Enterprises (Dunn and Bradstreet)
- Who Owns Whom (Dunn and Bradstreet)
- Sells' Scottish Directory
- Scotland's 2000 Companies
- Britain's Top Privately Owned Companies (Jordon)
- Institute membership handbooks – accountants, solicitors, architects, engineers, etc.
- UK Franchise Directory

- Willings Press Guide, UK – a directory of all newspapers and details thereof – owner, telephone number & address, circulation and geographic area etc.
- Brad – similar to the above
- Trade Associations and Professional Institutions in the UK – a directory of all such UK organisations (Gale Research International)
- Market Search (Arlington Management Publication)
- Market Surveys Index – a comprehensive index of survey reports on markets and trends
- Government funding for UK business (Kogan Page Ltd)
- The Guide to Venture Capital in the UK (Pitman)
- General Household Survey (Office of Population Census and Surveys)
- Family Expenditure Survey (Central Statistical Office)
- Census (HMSO)
- Encyclopaedia of Business Information Services
- Scavenger

Appendix D - Competitor's Record

Competitor's Name:			
Location:			
Geographic area of Trade:			
Number of employees:			
Date started business:			
	Last year	2nd year ago	3 years ago
Sales	£	£	£
Profits	£	£	£

Established in the geographic trading area?

Well   Quite well   Not very well

Reputation

Good   Quite good   Not very good

General comments on the business:

Comments on business expansion or contraction:

Comments on general business strengths or weaknesses:
Strengths:
Weaknesses:
Product(s) description:
Price: £
Assessment of quality:
Product's strengths:
Product's weaknesses:
Competitor's sales information on file ~ Yes

Appendix E - The Activity Plans

> "Financial planning" or "Forecasting" or "budgeting" involves more than simply an exercise in committing figures for future periods to paper. It is a process whereby management realistically considers the objectives and the steps needed to help achieve those aims."

The key attributes of activity planning are that it helps you to see:

- Clearly the tasks to be done
- The order in which they have to be completed
- When the tasks have to be completed by
- When too many activities are happening at once, thereby assisting in the division of tasks between people or planning arrangements

This example may be an example of a plan for establishing a small production factory.

LEVEL 1 ~ SUMMARY PLAN

Month	1	2	3	4	5	6	7	8	9	10	11	12
Business plan:												
Base	X	X										
Reviews		X	X		X			X			X	
Review/agree funding				X	X	X						
Choose premises				X	X							
Agree terms and lease					X	X						
Detail production plan					X							
Agree planning permission					X	X						
Building work							X	X	X			
Negotiate plant & equipment							X	X				
Plant installation									X	X		
Recruitment of staff:												
Sales							X	X				
Production									X	X		
Admin								X	X	X		
Advertising campaign									X	X	X	
Delivery of supplies										X		
Start manufacture									X	X		
First deliveries												X

LEVEL 2 PLAN ~ ADVERTISING CAMPAIGN

- Sales literature
- Customer Contact
- Trade Publications
- Samples
- Exhibitions
- Web-site

LEVEL 3 ~ SALES LITERATURE

- Initial Draft
- Copywriting
- Designing
  Artwork
  Proof
  Setting
  Plate making
  Proofs
  Agreement
  Printing

LEVEL 4 ~ INITIAL DRAFT

- First Draft
- Personal review and amendments
- Discuss
- Further review and amendments
- 'Final' agreement

You could combine levels 3 and 4 if you wish, even all of them – it's up to you to decide how you wish to organise the information. Below, I combine level's 2, 3 and 4 to show you how it would look.

LEVELS 2, 3 AND 4

- Sales Literature
  Initial Draft
  First draft
  Personal review and amendments
  Discuss
  Further review and amendments
  'Final' draft agreed
  Copywriting
  Designing
  Artwork
  Proof
  Setting
  Plate making
  Proofs
  Agreement
  Printing
- Customer Contact
- Insert in trade publications
- Samples
- Exhibitions

NO MATTER HOW THOROUGH YOU'RE PLANNING AND RESEARCH IT RARELY WORKS OUT AS THE PLAN SAYS.

YOU MUST BE FLEXIBLE, ABLE TO REORGANISE AND BE PATIENT.

YOU WILL HAVE TO MANAGE THE PROBLEMS.

BUT THIS IS NOT A REASON FOR NOT DOING YOUR PLANNING.

Appendix F -
Personal Financial Forecasting

INTRODUCTION

Personal cash forecasting is not complicated. You simply list your receipts and deduct your payments – and that's all there is to it!

If there is any 'difficulty', it is ensuring that you have included everything, and we give below many of the most common items to consider.

APPROACH

Spilt your income and expenditure across the following headings:

- Certain income
  Continued employment, pensions, continuing government benefits
- Uncertain income
  Overtime, a debt you are not sure will be repaid
- Unavoidable expenditure
  Basic food, clothing and housing etc
- Important expenditure
  Can be avoided but with difficulty
- Desirable expenditure
  Non-essential

We cannot say into which category of expenditure you should put any particular item. For example, a car to one person may be unavoidable expenditure, but to another it is important or even just desirable expenditure. Tobacco and alcohol may be important to some, desirable to others and so on.

With income and expenditure categorised in this manner you will quickly be able to calculate levels of survivability, it:

- Certain income less unavoidable expenditure
- Income less unavoidable and important expenditure

And so on. Thus, you can calculate by how much expenditure has to be reduced (if at all) or income increased to meet needs.

INFORMATION

We give below many of the items of income and expenditure that normally have to be considered.

INCOMES

- Debt repayment
- Investment dividends
- Interest
  Bank, building society, government securities
- Employment
  Temporary, fulltime, overtime, commissions and bonuses, gifts under a will
- Gifts of money
  Presents
- Government benefits
- Receipt from insurance claim
- Income from lodgers
- Maturity of savings policy PRPs
  Also mortgage endowment policies
- Pensions
  Employment, military, government
- Proceeds of something you are selling
- Rent
- Trust income
  also from covenants
- Termination settlement
  Redundancy, pension commutation
- Tax repayments

EXPENDITURE

- Housing

  Rent, mortgage, endowment policy, building insurance, repayment insurance, contents insurance, maintenance, freezer insurance

- Community Tax
- Utilities

  Electricity, gas, water, coal, telephone

- Other insurances

  Medical, recreation (boats, etc)

- Vehicle

  Petrol, oil, maintenance, insurance, road fund tax, tyres, loan repayments

- Debt payments

  Credit cards, bank loans, shop accountants, lending companies, instalment and hire purchase tax

- Rentals

  TV, Video, cam-recorder, satellite

- Travel

  Season tickets, rail, tube, taxis

- Household

  Chemist, cleaning, household materials, magazines and papers

- Food

  Milk, groceries, fruit and vegetables, meat and fish

- Personal

  Hair, cosmetics, clothes, dentist, toiletries

- Pets

  Food, vets, insurance

- Children

  Pocket money, school extras and trips

- Presents

  Birthday, Christmas, anniversaries

- Other

  Tobacco, charities, savings, holidays, professional subscriptions, parties and entertainment, garden, alcohol, savings clubs, club memberships, theatre, cinema, hobbies, sport, equipment and furniture

POINTS TO CONSIDER
General points

- Prepare the forecast for at least 12 months
- Check when incomes and expenses cease during the period of the forecast
- Remember that if a month end balance is only just positive the balance may have been in overdraft during the month

Opening debts and outstanding invoices?

- What unpaid invoices are there?
- What arrears are owed?
- Do any debt repayment plans finish in the period?
- Although not a direct consideration in most cases what net assets are there available for disposal to pay debts?
- What assets are available as security?

Income

- When are increases and bonuses due?
- Are all government benefits being claimed?

Expenses

- Allow for increases in cost for inflation and increases from renewal fate of policies

PERSONAL FINANCIAL FORECAST FORMAT

Because the detail varies in each individual case we only provide an outline of the format

		Jan	Feb	Mar	Apr	May	Jun	⇒
Weeks ⇒		4	4	5	4	4	5	
		£	£	£	£	£	£	
Balance brought forward	(a)							
Certain income								
Item								
Item								
Total certain income	(b)							
Uncertain income								
Item								
Item								
Total uncertain income	(c)							
Total income	(d=b+c)							
Unavoidable expenditure								
Item								
Item								
Total unavoidable expenditure	(e)							
Important expenditure								
Item								
Item								
Total important expenditure	(f)							
Desirable expenditure								
Item								
Item								
Total desirable expenditure	(g)							
TOTAL EXPENDITURE	(h=e+f+g)							
BALANCE CARRIED FORWARD	(a+d−h)							

- **ENTER RECEIPTS AND PAYMENTS IN THE MONTH IN WHICH YOU EXPECT TO RECEIVE AND PAY THE AMOUNT.**

- **PREPARE FIRST AND AGREE A STATEMENT THAT INCLUDES ALL INCOME AND EXPENDITURE, THEN THOSE FOR THE DIFFERENT LEVELS OF SURVIVABILITY.**

- **INCLUDE A LINE AT LEAST FOR EVERY MAIN CATEGORY OF INCOME AND EXPENDITURE – DO NOT LUMP ITEMS TOGETHER IF IT CAN BE A AVOIDED; DO DETAILED CALCULATIONS SEPARATELY IF NECESSARY**

- **KEEP NOTES OF THE UNDERLYING ASSUMPTIONS – FOR EXAMPLE, IF YOU ASSUME AN INCREASE IN AN INCOME FROM SOME FUTURE DATE NOTE THE BASIS ON WHICH IT IS CALCULATED**

- **WHERE APPROPRIATE CALCULATE INCOME AND EXPENDITURE ACCORDING TO THE ACTUAL NUMBER OF WEEKS IN THE MONTH**

Appendix G - Accounting Terms and Principles

This section briefly explains the accounting terms and principles found in basic financial recording and reporting. Words in CAPITALS are defined elsewhere in the booklet.

The purpose is to introduce the concepts in a general way to those not familiar with them, rather than writing yet another accounting textbook! In striving, therefore, to present the principles clearly some points have been simplified or ignored.

Points will become clearer when you go through the worked example MYBIZ and see the theory working in practice.

✻ ✻ ✻ ✻ ✻ ✻ ✻ ✻ ✻

**AN ACCOUNT or
LEDGER account – A/C**

A record of the DEBIT and CREDIT transactions of a like nature; accounts may be 'opened' in a LEDGER to record any particular type of FINANCIAL TRANSACTION – as examples:

**Electricity – Vehicles – Travel – Tax
Rent – PURCHASES – DEBTORS
SALES – bank – CREDITORS
furniture and fittings – telephone
entertaining**

A business MUST open accounts to record certain transactions required by law, for example an account to record the VAT element of transactions if it is registered for VAT.

Accounts are opened to provide financial information and as long as the business complies with legal requirements it may record and report its financial transactions in any way it chooses to provide the information its managers need to run the business.

Accounts are traditionally represented as follows and known as 'T' accounts because of the way the lines are drawn:

DEBITS		CREDITS	
Date	**£**	**Date**	**£**
ASSETS		LIABILITIES	
COSTS		INCOMES	
RECEIPTS		PAYMENTS	
LOSSES		PROFITS	
Total		**Total**	

ACCOUNT BALANCE

The difference in the totals of the DEBIT entries and CREDIT entries in an ACCOUNT.

DEBITS		CREDITS	
	£		£
	100		300
	120	Balance carried down - Bal. c/d	420
	500		
	720		720
Bal.b/d	420		

Note that the 'balancing' entry of £420 has to go on the credit side of the account to make the two totals agree; this means that the total of the debit entries was greater than the total of the credit entries before the balancing figure was entered; thus the account balance is a debit balance.

With the advent of computer accounting it has become common to present 'debits and credits' in a column with one or other shown as a negative figure. Thus the above account could also be represented as follows:

	£
	100
	120
	500
	-300
Balance	420
or	
	100
	120
	500
	-300
Balance	-420
	0

ACCOUNTING PERIOD

This is simply the time interval reflected in a financial report or some other accounting activity and may be as long or as short as the managers of a business require. Thus, it may be for a week, month, quarter, bi-annual or year. It may, however, be as short as an hour, for example, an hourly report on cash takings in a large department store.

Often financial reporting is for a year with interim monthly and quarterly report; a LIMITED COMPANY MUST, in normal circumstances, produce a SET OF ACCOUNTS for a twelve month period.

The financial year is the date to which the annual set of accounts is made up, e.g. the twelve months to 31st December (see CUT-OFF-DATE).

ACCRUALS

A Type of LIABILITY and the opposite to a PREPAYMENT, an accrual is calculated by the business for an EXPENSE that is correctly chargeable for an ACCOUNTING PERIOD but which has not yet been invoiced to the business:

- A business makes up its accounts to 31st March and the invoice for the quarter's charge for the telephone will next be received at the end of April. An accrual should be included in the accounts to 31st March for the estimated charge for use in January and February yet to be billed.

- If the business were to go into LIQUIDATION on the 31st March it would owe the telephone company the charges for January and February.

Accruals are entered in the GENERAL JOURNAL before being posted to the GENERAL LEDGER.

ASSET

Something owned by or owed to the business, for example:

- A Building
- An item of machinery
- A DEBT
- A positive bank balance, i.e. in hand, owed by the bank to the business
- STOCKS of materials or finished goods

AUDIT

An independent inspection by those acting on behalf of a third party into the correctness and fairness of a set of records and/or SET OF ACCOUNTS.

A Financial audit of the STATUTORY ACCOUNTS is often, and in some cases has to be, undertaken on behalf of the shareholders or partners in a business; other audits are carried out on behalf of government agencies on such matters as:

- Pay As You Earn, Corporation Tax – the Inland Revenue
- Value Added Tax – Customs and Excise
- Health and Safety issues – Health and Safety Executive

BALANCE
See ACCOUNT BALANCE

BANK RECONCILIATION

A business is certain to open a CASH BOOK, a DAY BOOK to record its RECEIPTS and PAYMENTS. Similarly, a bank will open an account with the business and will 'mirror' reflect the entries the business makes, that is, the opposite way round.

For example, if the business pays £100 into the bank it will record a receipt in its cash book and the bank will show a liability in its account with the business because it owes the business £100 – the business will be 'in credit' at the bank. (The bank also keeps a cash book and it will have recorded a receipt of £100 in it from the business).

There is often a timing difference between when an entry is made in the business' cash book and when it is made by the bank:

- The business may pay a cheque to a supplier who does not 'bank it' for several weeks
- A bank charge is entered by the bank on the business' account but which is not yet entered in the cash book
- The business has entered a receipt in the cash book which is not yet credited by the bank

A bank reconciliation is prepared to check the business' records against those of the bank simply by comparing the entries in one set of records with those in the other set. If proper adjustment is made for 'missing entries' the adjust BALANCES should be the same.

Example:
Suppose the cash book of **MYBIZ** shows the following Entries:

DEBITS		CREDITS	
	£		£
RECEIPTS	100	PAYMENTS	20
	300		200
	250		50
	750		100
		Balance c/d	1030
	–1400		1400
Balance b/d	1030		

MYBIZ's entries in the books of the bank are given below. Remember, they are the opposite way round to the presentation in MYBIZ's cash book; the bank owes the amounts to the business paid in as receipts and is owed for the payments it has made on behalf of the business

DEBITS		CREDITS	
	£		£
Payments made on behalf of business	20	Receipts received from the business	100
	200		300
	50		250
Bank charges	10		
Balance c/d	370		
	650		650
		Balance b/d	370

The reconciliation between the two sets of records is prepared by adjusting each BALANCE for the missing entries:

	MYBIZ £	BANK £
Balance	1030	370
Missing entries:		
Add receipt in MYBIZ's cash book not in bank account		750
Deduct payments in MYBIZ's cash book not in bank account		(100)
Deduct bank charges in bank account not in MYBIZ's cash book	(10)	
Adjusted balances	1020	1020

MYBIZ must enter the bank charges in its cash book; the bank will enter the missing receipt as soon as its systems allow and the missing payment shortly after the supplier pays the cheque into the bank.

Thus the two sets of records are in agreement after allowing for the reconciling entries.

When the business' balance in the bank's books is a DEBIT balance it is overdrawn i.e. the business owes the bank the balance. Likewise, the cash book balance is said to be overdrawn when I is a CREDIT balance.

SHAREHOLDERS	£	£
CAPITAL	x	
Accumulated PROFITS	x	
RESERVES	x	
		x
LONG TERM LIABILITIES		x
CURRENT LIABILITIES		
Trade CREDITORS	x	
Taxes	x	
Bank Overdraft	x	
		x
Total LIABILITIES		x

*Work in progress

BUDGET

Managers discuss and agree an accepted assessment of future results to strive for, for example of cash RECEIPTS and PAYMENTS, INCOMES, COSTS, PROFITS and BALANCE SHEETS and this base position becomes the budget. Once it is agreed it never changes. (See FORECASTS).

A budget does not have to be just for financial results; for example, it can be of future levels of:

BALANCE SHEETS – B/S

A set of STATUTORY ACCOUNTS includes a PROFIT AND LOSS ACCOUNT and a balance sheet. The Profit and Loss Account shows the results of trading, of carrying on business FOR a period of time, for a month or for a quarter and son on – INCOME less EXPENSES. (See ACCOUNTING PERIOD).

A balance sheet, a financial report, shows what the business owns and owes AT a particular point in time. It summarises the ASSETS and LIABILITIES of a business at a particular date and traditionally looks like this:

FIXED ASSETS	£	£
COST	x	
less DEPRECIATION	x	
		x
CURRENT ASSETS		
STOCKS and WIP*	x	
DEBTORS	x	
Bank and Cash	x	
		x
Total ASSETS		x

- Personal
- Numbers of items of STOCKS and finished goods

CAPITALS

The amount put into the business by the owner or owners – usually in cash but not necessarily; sometimes it is in the form of ASSETS, for example, in STOCK or equipment.

In the case of a LIMITED COMPANY capital

is represented by SHARES issued by it to the shareholders as evidence of the amount they have invested. NOMINAL SHARE CAPITAL can take several forms and the most common types are ORDINARY and PREFERENCE. The rights and obligations attaching to each class of share are given in the company's Memorandum and Articles of Association.

In the case of a SOLE TRADER or PARTNERSHIP capital is the reflection of the ASSETS and LIABILITIES of their business and is not represented by shares as such.

In the case of a partnership each partner owns a proportion of the NET ASSETS of the business according to a ratio agreed by the partners. A sole trader owns all of the net assets.

CASH BOOK

The term 'cash' is used to denote coin and cheques and the cash book is a DAY BOOK which records the RECEIPTS paid into a bank account and the PAYMENTS made from it.

The BALANCE at any one time may be either a DEBIT (in hand) or CREDIT (overdrawn) and represents the business' position with the bank.

The bank therefore will be either a DEBTOR or CREDITOR of the business depending on which the balance is, and the only distinction between it and an account with another business is that in this case the balance represents money rather than goods and services bought and sold.

Sometimes a business will receive and pay small amounts in coin which do not involve the bank and these are recorded in petty cash book.

Because of its importance the cash book balance is shown separately on the BALANCE SHHET under the heading bank and cash. Do not be confused – although the description used includes the work 'bank' this means the balance with the bank in the business' cash book AND NOT the balance in the bank's books. (See BANK RECONCILIATION)

Just like any other day book the cash book may be used to analyse transactions, and the totals will be POSTED in the GENERAL LEDGER to the cash book CONTROL ACCOUNT. The balance in the cash book should be the same as in the control account at the end of the ACCOUNTING PERIOD.

CASH FLOW

A financial report shows, in as much or as little detail as needed, PAYMENTS RECEIPTS and the resulting difference. Reports may show what happened in the past or be a BUDGET or FORECAST of the future – all usually providing information on a monthly basis.

CLOSING THE ACCOUNTS AT THE END OF THE ACCOUNTING PERIOD

At the end of the ACCOUNTING PERIOD, and after all adjustments (see GENERAL JOURNAL) have been made, there will be BALANCES on each of the INCOME and EXPENSE accounts and ASSET and LIABILITY accounts.

The balances on the income and expenses accounts are transferred by journal entry to the PROFIT AND LOSS ACCOUNT; similarly the assets and liabilities are transferred to the BALANCE SHEET. The 'full closure' of accounts normally only takes place at the end of the financial year, when the 'annual accounts' are prepared. The closing balances on the balance sheet are carried forward to start the next accounting period and the posting process starts over again.

There will be no income and expense balances carried forward to the next accounting period. They were transferred to the profit and loss account in the last period and the net profit (or loss) for the period was included in the balance sheet as one of the opening balances brought forward, usually in accumulated profits. (See BALANCE SHEET).

CONTROL ACCOUNT

An ACCOUNT in a LEDGER, usually the GENERAL LEDGER, that records the total of all FINANCIAL TRANSACTIONS in a DAY BOOK or other ledger.

CONVENTIONS

There are a number of assumptions and influences – conventions – that are considered when preparing a SET OF ACCOUNTS or in understanding them. The most important are as follows:

- ACCOUNTING PERIOD – a set of accounts present the results of the business in financial terms for an ACCOUNTING PERIOD, a month, quarter, year or whatever, and at a point in time (see PROFIT AND LOSS ACCOUNT and BALANCE SHEET).

- Matching – INCOMES and EXPENSES must be matched to each other in the same and appropriate period. If a sale is made on the 31st March the expense of the sale must also be included in the accounts to the 31st March matching expense with income; expenditure related to sales in April must not be included in the previous year's Profit and Loss Accounts (see ACCRUALS, PREPAYMENTS and CUT-FF)

- Historic cost – FINANCIAL TRANSACTIONS are recorded in the LEDGERS at the amount of the transaction when it occurs. Thus, if an item is sold for £100 in April it will also be reported as a SALE of £100 in the Profit and Loss Account for the financial year ending on the 31st March, almost a year after the transaction took place – that is, without any adjustment for inflation over the year. In times of high inflation attempts have been made to reflect the effect of inflation,

called Current Cost Accounting.

- Consistency – the comparison of the results for one accounting period with another only makes sense if all the transactions are recorded and reported in the same manner for each period. There are legitimate reasons for changing the way in which transactions are reported and previous results may then have to be 'restated' to make any comparison meaningful.

- Prudence – a business must NOT take PROFIT into an accounting period unless it has been earned, it has actually arisen; it must, however, provided for a LOSS that is going to take place in the future as soon as it is known it will happen. CURRENT ASSETS and LIABILITIES should only be included in the balance sheet at the VALUES they are expected to be received or paid for in cash

- Objectivity – a set of accounts must be a fair and honest representation of the reality of doing business over a period of time and at a particular date

- Materiality – the accounts must fairly represent all key information on INCOME and EXPENSES, ASSESTS and LIABILITIES needed for an understanding of the business covered by the period of the accounts; conversely it should not include detail unnecessary for that understanding

- It is permissible to group information under one heading in a set of accounts as long as any analysis required to be given by law is shown elsewhere, for example in NOTES TO THE ACCOUNTS.

COST

The DEBIT entry reflecting a PAYMENT, CREDITOR of ACCRUAL transaction; costs may be for;

- An ASSET that is purchased – buildings, machinery, computers
- Or an EXPENSE which may be:
  OVERHEAD EXPENSES – travel, telephone, audit fees, electricity, DEPRECIATION
  DIRECT EXPENSES – product PURCHASES and other expenses related specifically to making the product or providing the service
  Often the term 'cost' is used in place of expense

CREDIT – CR for short

An entry on the right hand side of an ACCOUNT, from the Latin meaning a loan.

CREDITOR

Someone or some business to whom the business owes money – often an invoice will have been received, e.g. in respect of PURCHASES from a trade supplier. When a PAYMENT is made to creditor cash goes down and creditors go down.

CURRENT ASSETS

Those ASSETS which arise as a result of or become of trading, doing business, for example:

- STOCKS of materials
- WORK-IN-PROGRESS
- Finished Goods
- DEBTORS and PREPAYMENTS
- Bank and cash BALANCES in hand

Current assets are sometimes called circulating assets because as the business process takes place they change their nature:

- Stocks of materials are turned into work-in-progress

- Work-in-progress is turned into finished goods
- Finished goods are sold and turned into debtors (if the goods are not paid for immediately) or cash (if they are paid for at once)
- Debtors are turned into cash when payment is made
- The cash is then used to pay CREDITORS for more stocks of materials

And the process continues in a seamless activity

CURRENT LIABILITIES

Like CURRENT ASSETS, current liabilities arise through the business process and are amounts owed by the business and due for payment within a year, for example, amounts owed to:

- Trade CREDITORS for PURCHASES
- ACCRUALS
- The government in one form or other for taxes
- The bank if the balance is overdrawn

Amounts not due for payment within a year are called LONG TERM LIABILITIES.

CUT-OFF DATE

The cut-off date is the end of the ACCOUNTING PERIOD to which is SET OF ACCOUNTS is drawn up. It is important to consider the matching CONVENTION and the concept of ACCRUALS and PREPAYMENTS and SALES reserves and PURCHASE reserves at this date.

If a business' financial year end (see ACCOUNTING PERIOD) is 31st March and it physically takes receipt of STOCK on that date but does not pay for it until the following year it must create an entry to represent the ASSET and LIABILITY – in this case, possession of the stock with the obligation to pay for it.

DAY BOOKS – also called DAY JOURNALS

It will be appreciated that a business may incur many transactions each day, many of them of like nature; the principal ones are in respect of SALES, COSTS and cash – in this last case the cash day book is usually known simply as the CASH BOOK, which records the receipt of cheques as well as hard cash paid into the bank.

By their nature many of these FINANCIAL TRANSACTIONS would be POSTED to the same ACCOUNT and it became the practice to enter the day's transactions in a day book and then transfer the totals to the appropriate CONTROL ACCOUNTS in the GENERAL LEDGER at periodic intervals – rather than entering each transaction separately in the general ledger account.

Thus, there is usually a SALES day book, a COSTS day book and a cash (day) book to record all the prime entries, that is, books in which a financial transaction is first (prime) recorded. The cost day book may be further divided into sections for EXPENSES and FIXED ASSETS, and the former further divided into DIRECT and INDIRECT expenses. Normally, the totals of the day books are posted to the general ledger and subsidiary ledgers at the end of the ACCOUNTING PERIOD. (See GENERAL JOURNAL).

The payroll can be regarded for practical terms as a day book giving rise to totals that are posted to the general ledger with payments subsequently made through the cash book. Payroll expenses may be either direct or indirect.

A day book's other purpose is to analyze the transactions, thus sales can be analyzed by nature of sale, expenses by nature of expense and so on. A sales day book may look like the following.

Date to whom sold		Total	Product Analysis of Sales			
			A	B	C	D
		£	£	£	£	£
1.1	Mr A	100	100			
1.1	Mr B	200		200		
1.1	Mr C	300		300		
1.1	Mr D	400				400
		1000	100	500		400

The entries in the GENERAL LEDGER would be to POST £1000 in the DEBTORS' CONTROL ACCOUNT (assuming the sales were not for cash) and in the Sales Control Account:

	£	£
Dr - Debtor's Control a/c	1000	
Cr - Sales Control a/c		1000

Separate entries would be made in the Debtor's Ledger (see LEDGER) showing Mr A with a balance of £100, Mr B with a balance of £200 and so on.

The term day book is often replaced by 'analysis', especially in a computer accounting system – sales analysis, purchase analysis.

DEBIT - DR for short

An entry on the left hand side of an ACCOUNT, from the Latin meaning a debt.

DEBT

The term can be used to denote an amount owning by the business and to the business depending on its use.

DEBTOR

Someone or some business who owes something, usually money, to the business. When a debtor pays his invoice cash goes up and debtors go down.

DEPRECIATION

A FIXED ASSET benefits a business for a number of ACCOUNTING PERIODS, until the asset is not longer of use. Thus, a lorry may cost £10,000 and may be expected to last 5 years; each year's PROFITS should be charged with £2000 and the COST of the van reduced by £2000 each year to reflect the use the business has had of the van in that year – depreciation is the cost of using a fixed asset for a period of time. The cost of a fixed asset less accumulated depreciation also represents the estimated VALUE of the asset after a period of time. The cost of a fixed asset less its accumulated depreciation to date is known as the net book VALUE of the asset. The cost is said to be 'fully written off' when the accumulated depreciation equals the original cost and, all the things being equal, this should be at the end of the assets useful life. Depreciation is an example of the matching CONVENTION.

Depreciation results in a DEBIT entry to the PROFIT AND LOSS ACCOUNT – an expense – and a CREDIT entry to the Provision for Depreciation Account.

Depreciation also has the effect of putting aside other assets of the business to replace a fixed asset at the end of its useful life. Supplement 3 explains this but we suggest you read it only when confident with the rest of the booklet.

Sometimes fixed assets appreciate in VALUE, that is increase, most usually a freehold building. In this case the net book value is increased to the estimated value and the difference, the profit, transferred to a RESERVE account. This profit is not take to the P & L account because it does not arise from trading.

There are several ways in which depreciation can be calculated, dependent upon the nature of the business and the asset being depreciated.

DIRECT EXPENSE

A direct expense is on that can be allocated directly to the product, service, process or project itself. It relates directly to making the product or providing the service and includes such items are:

- Product parts and materials and other PURCHASES
- Wages and salaries to make or perform the product or service
- Delivery costs from suppliers and to customers
- Product testing

A share of INDIRECT EXPENSES may also be apportioned to each product or service to determine true profitability. (See EXPENSE ALLOCATION).

DOUBLE ENTRY ACCOUNTING

The standard method of recording FINANCIAL TRANSACTIONS, are those following Western accounting traditions. There is no fundamental reason why DEBITS are on the left of an ACCOUNT and the CREDITS on the right; that's just the way we have got used to it.

Each financial transaction is recorded twice:

- Once in an ACCOUNT showing what the affect is to the business – INCOME and COSTS

- Once in an account showing what the effect is to the outside world – DEBTORS, CREDITORS, BANK, SHAREHOLDERS

Every debit MUST have a credit and every credit MUST have a debit! Recording an entry is call POSTING an entry.

This may be better understood by a few examples:

- The business pays for a van of £5000 by cheque; it records the van as an ASSET, A DEBIT, because it owns the van and the PAYMENT as a LIABILITY, A CREDIT, because it owes the bank the money used to purchase the van. The entries would be entered in tow accounts:

- The business sells some goods for £1000 for cash and banks for the amount – it records the RECEIPT of cash as an ASSET, A DEBIT, because it is owed the cash by the bank and the SALE as a CREDIT, a LIABILITY – all other things being equal this is a PROFIT that the business owes to the owners

- The business owes £300 for a telephone bill – it records the EXPENSE as a DEBIT, and the LIABILITY as a CREDIT because it owes the money to a CREDITOR, the telephone company.

DRAWINGS

The amount taken out of the business or partnership by the owner(s) – the equivalent of a salary in respect of employment in a LIMITED COMPANY.

EQUITY

Another term for the shareholder's or owner's financial interest (share) in the business – his or their ownership in it.

EXPENSE

A COST to the business other than for a FIXED ASSET. An expense in respect of a delivery of goods is known as a PURCHASE. The term expense is often used instead of cost and vice versa.

EXPENSE ALLOCATION

All but the simplest of businesses will offer different products and services and the managers will want to know which 'line' is profitable and which isn't. Expense allocation is the manner in which the business EXPENSES are apportioned to determine product/project/process/service profitability. In principle, there are two types of expense to be apportioned:

- DIRECT EXPENSES
- INDIRECT EXPENSES

To determine the true cost of a product or service not only will direct expenses be allocated to it but indirect expense as well, in accordance with some formula. In this way total expenses of the business will have been apportioned to the products and services.

A common way, but by no means the only way, is by charging each product or service with a share of indirect expenses in proportion to the amount of direct payroll expense involved in producing that product or service. For example, indirect expenses totalling £5,000 would be apportioned as follows:

	Product		
	A	**B**	**Total**
	£	£	£
Direct Labour	**1500**	**2500**	**4000**
Indirect Expenses	**185**	**3125**	**5000**

$$£\frac{1500}{4000} \times 5000 \qquad £\frac{2500}{4000} \times 5000$$

See also **MANAGEMENT ACCOUNTS**

FINANCIAL TRANSACTION - ACCOUNTING ENTRY

Business decisions give rise to a result that can be represented in money terms and these financial transactions are recorded in a SET OF BOOKS.

There are ALWAYS two halves to a financial transaction – a DEBIT and a CREDIT.

See DOUBLE ENTRY ACCOUNTING.

Normally a transaction will be evidenced by a piece of paper or papers; examples:

- A purchase by a supplier's invoice
- A sale by a sales invoice
- A lease by an agreement

Financial transactions must be coded, that is, given a reference that identifies the ACCOUNT to which it is to be POSTED. It is vital that the correct code is assigned – if not the transaction will be posted to the incorrect account and subsequent reported information will be wrong – the picture will be blurred!

Financial transactions must be authorised, that is, agreed by the appropriate level of management, before the transaction occurs.

FIXED ASSET – also CAPITAL ASSET

A FIXED ASSET is a COST to the business that will benefit it over a number of ACCOUNTING PERIODS, for example:

- A building
- Plant and machinery
- A vehicle
- A computer

The business does not 'trade' in these assets, rather they are acquired to carry on the business – they are the fabric or infrastructure of the business. Their cost is charged to PROFITS by creating a DEPRESIATION provision. The cost of a fixed asset less its accumulated depreciation to date is known as the net book VALUE of that asset.

FORECAST

As the actual results, for example SALES become known they are compared to the BUDGET. A reassessment may then be made of the future – this is a forecast:

		Actual Results £	December Budget £	Year End Forecast £
Cumulative sales to:	March	4000	15000	15000
	June	9000	15000	18000
	Septemmber	14000	15000	19000
	December	18500	15000	–

A forecast may be assessed for anything this is budgeted.

GENERAL JOURNAL

The DAY BOOKS are the normal books of prime entry – where a FINANCIAL TRANSACTION is first recorded – for COSTS and INCOMES, the CASH BOOK and payroll. However, some accounting entries are needed which do not naturally originate from a prime entry entered in a day book, for example, entries to:

- Correct other entries which are wrong
- CLOSE THE ACCOUNTS at the end of the ACCOUNTING PERIOD
- Create a SALE and PURCHASE reserves
- Create a CAPITAL RESERVE
- Create a PROVISION, for example, for DEPRECIATION or for bad debts
- Create ACCRUALS and PREPAYMENTS
- Record GOODWILL

They are adjustments and such entries are commonly known as journal entries and entered in the general journal before being POSTED to the appropriate ACCOUNTS. Each entry should have a clear description explaining why it is required.

GENERAL LEDGER

The general ledger is the LEDGER that records all the FINANCIAL TRANSACTIONS of the business, either at individual transaction level or at CONTROL ACCOUNT level. It is the summary ledger and when all transactions have been POSTED the TRIAL BALANCE is prepared from it to prove that all 'accounts are in balance'.

GOODWILL

Goodwill is an ASSET of the company that often does not appear in the BALANCE SHEET. For example, suppose the business shown in SHARE ASSET VALUE has been going for a number of years and has built up a good reputation, has a loyal workforce and customer base, a good product range, is profitable and so on, these 'intangibles' (something you cannot touch) are worth something but are not shown on the balance sheet. This additional VALUE is known as goodwill. Thus, if someone wanted to buy the business and was prepared to pay £5 per share he would in effect be valuing the goodwill at £2 per share (that is, £2 more than the asset value per share). Goodwill arises in the same way in a PARTNERSHIP and a SOLE TRADER'S business.

Its value is entered in the GENERAL LEDGER by an entry POSTED from the GENERAL JOURNAL.

GROSS PROFIT (LOSS)

Gross profit is SALES less DIRECT EXPENSES; it is also sometimes known as the trading profit, and is arrived at before deduction of INDIRECT EXPENSES, tax, dividends, and DRAWINGS. (See PROFIT AND LOSS ACCOUNT.)

INCOME

An amount earned by the business, for example, SALES or interest income. If it is not yet paid to the business the other entry is a DEBIT to DEBTORS. When paid the RECEIPT will be entered in the CASH BOOK as a DEBIT, because the cash ASSET has increased and the CREDIT side of the transaction will be POSTED to the debtor account to eliminate the debt.

INCORPORATION

The legal and operational process of forming a LIMITED COMPANY. A company cannot trade; carry on business, until it has been issued with a trading certificate.

INDIRECT EXPENSE – OVERHEADS

Indirect Expenses are those which cannot be attributed directly (see DIRECT EXPENSE) to making the product or delivering the service. They include such items as:

Rent – rates – general expenses – audit fee – bank charges – office – salaries and wages – stationery – entertaining

To determine the real profitability of a product or service, indirect expenses are apportioned to the products or services in accordance with some agreed principal of allocation. (See EXPENSE ALLOCATION).

LEDGER

Another name for a book in which FINANCIAL TRANSACTIONS are recorded. The summary ledger is called the GENERAL LEDGER.

Often a ledger is opened for a particular type of transaction, usually when there are a substantial number of them, such as a:

- FIXED ASSET ledger – details of all the fixed assets the business owns
- DEBTORS ledger – details of all those who owe the business money and how much

- CREDITORS ledger – similar to the debtors' ledger but for amounts owing by the business
- DIRECT EXPENSE ledger – one that records the direct expenses including PURCHASES by product etc.
- INDIRECT EXPENSES ledger – one that records indirect expenses

These are often known as subsidiary ledgers, and the totals of the transactions they contain will be entered in CONTROL ACCOUNTS in the general ledger. If all entries have POSTED correctly, the total of all BALANCES in a subsidiary ledger will be the same as the balance on the appropriate control account. For example, the total of all the individual debtor's account in the debtor's ledger should be the same as the balance on the Debtors' Control Account in the general ledger.

LIABILITY

Amounts owed by the business to someone else or to some other business, for example:

- To trade CREDITORS for DIRECT and INDIRECT EXPENSES taken on credit i.e. not paid for on delivery. The use of the word trade simply distinguishes those creditors from whom you buy goods and services and those such as the bank, SHAREHOLDERS, government.
- CAPITAL owed by the business to those who provided it to the business
- PROFITS made by the business owed to the owners. i.e. shareholders PARTNERS or SOLE TRADER
- An overdrawn bank balance owed to the bank by the business
- An ACCRUAL

LIMITED COMPANY

An INCORPORATED organisation whereby the LIABILITY of those providing the CAPITAL is limited to the amount of money they originally paid into it. (See LIQUIDATION).

There are two main types:

- A private limited company where the SHARE are not bought and sold by the public on a stock exchange
- A public limited company where the shares are traded by the public on a stock exchange

LIMITED LIABILITY

The concept of limited liability is important because of the underlying principle involved, namely that a LIMITED COMPANY is a separate person in law, separate from those owning it, and responsible for its own affairs, conducted through its agents, the Directors and other officers of the company. In the case of a PARTNERSHIP or a SOLE TRADER the partners and the individual are the business and inseparable from it. The business' liability is their liability. In the case of a limited company it, being a separate person, is responsible for its own debtors.

In the case of a limited company the liability of a SHAREHOLDER to pay for the debts of a company is limited to the amount of CAPITAL he has paid into the company, evidenced by SHARES (in the form a share certificate). Thus, if shareholders initially subscribed a share capital of £10,000 and the company goes 'bust' owning CREDITORS £30,000 the creditors have no further redress to the shareholders whose liability is limited to the £10,000 thy initially paid in. (See LIQUIDATION).

In the case of the partners in a partnership or a sole trader the liability for the business' debts is unlimited and they may be required to sell personal assets to pay the creditors, for example, savings and investments, a car, or other personal assets.

LIQUIDATION

The process by which a LIMITED COMPANY is closed down, usually, but not always, when it cannot pay its CREDITORS what it owes them. A liquidator is appointed who sells all the assets, collects any debts owing to the business and pays off as much as possible to the creditors. If there is insufficient cash to pay all that is owning the liquidator cannot normally ask for more cash from the SHAREHOLDERS. Should there be funds left over after payment of all debts the balance will be paid to the shareholders according to their rights expressed in the MEMORANDUM AND ARTICLES OF ASSOIATION.

There is a special order in which creditors are paid, for example, takes, wages due to employees and debts secured on the general assets of the business are paid in full (funds permitting) before the unsecured creditors. If there is still cash left in the kitty the PREFERENCE shareholders will have their capital repaid; finally the ORDINARY shareholders will have what is left.

LONG TERM LIABILITIES

Amounts due for payment after a year, for example:

- Lease payments on a long lease due more than one year's hence
- Contract payments received in advance of work being done on long term contracts

LOSS

A loss arises when the total of all EXPENSES related to a particular event or ACCOUNTING PERIOD are greater than the INCOME for that event or period. For example, a loss results from trading over a period of time or from an event such as the disposal of a FIXED ASSET.

MANAGEMENT ACCOUNTS

Management accounts are prepared to assist managers in making business decisions by analyzing the historic results (see CONVENTIONS, historic cost) presented in a PROFIT AND LOSS ACCOUNT, and BUDGETING and FORECASTING future results.

Past and future analysis can take many forms including:

- Profit and Loss Account and BALANCE SHEET
- CASH FLOW analysis
- Cost and product analysis
  Departmental and activity costs
  Product costs, sales and profitability
  Project costs, sales and profitability
  Process costs, sales and profitability
- Labour use and efficiency
  Productive, non-productive time
- Operational efficiency
  Waste, faulty goods, rate of production
- Customer knowledge
  Sales
  Orders

There is no statutory requirement to keep any form of management accounts but it is difficult to see how any organisation of any size and complexity can function without such form of information. Indeed, it may be that directors cannot fulfil their statutory obligations without some form of management reporting.

What form financial management reporting rakes will depend on the nature and complexity of the business, and is, to some extent, a subjective matter – it depends on what information managers believe they need.

FINANCIAL TRANSACTIONS may not only be coded to a LEDGER ACCOUNT, but also given a second reference so that analysis can be prepared for the purposes of management accounts, for example, product profitability, a departmental expense report.

The analysis provided in a set of management accounts must agree to the totals represented in the normal statutory format:

	Statutory 'P&L'	Management Accounts Products		
		A	**B**	**C**
	£	£	£	£
SALES	1000	3000	5000	2000
LESS				
Materials	(2500)	(1000)	(1200)	(300)
Labour	(3000)	(300)	(2000)	(700)
GROSS PROFIT	4500	1700	1800	1000
INDIRECT EXPENSES	(3000)	(300)	(2000)	(700)
NET PROFIT/(LOSS)	1500	1400	(200)	300

MEMORANDUM and ARTICLES OF ASSOCIATION

A company is formed, INCORPORATED, for a particular purpose; this and how it is to operate to achieve the purpose are laid out in these two documents.

A model set of documents is provided by law but they may be altered for any proper reason; they include such matters as:

- The company's name
- Its registered address
- The purpose of the company
- Arrangements for meetings
- Appointment of directors
- Details of its NOMINAL SHARE CAPITAL, (the total capital it is allowed to issue)
- Rights of shareholders
- Transfer of shares

A company MUST operate within the provisions of the Memorandum and Articles of Association. In a PARTNERSHIP the equivalent 'rules' are defined in the partnership agreement. There is no equivalent for a SOLE TRADER.

NET ASSETS

The written down value of FIXED ASSETS (the COST of fixed assets less accumulated DEPRECIATION) plus NET CURRENT ASSETS less LONG TERM LIABILITIES. (See SHARE ASSET VALUE).

NET CURRENT ASSETS

The total of CURRENT ASSETS less the total of CURRENT LIABILITIES.
This is also known as:

- Net workings capital

or

- Net liquid assets – 'liquid' is a term used to describe assets and liabilities that are turned into cash, in the course of trading. (See CURRENT ASSETS.)

NOMINAL SHARE VALUE

The monetary unit value of one SHARE – its basic (nominal) unit value:

- ORDINARY SHARES of a nominal value of £1 means that the investor was/is obligated to pay a pound for each share he was/is allotted when the shares were/are first issued. This is not necessarily, indeed not usually after a period of time, the SHARE'S VALUE.
- Share are normally paid for in cash (see CAPITAL)
- PREFERENCE SHARES also have a nominal share value
- The nominal value of a share can be any value but is often 50p or a £1. The total nominal share capital of a LIMITED COMPANY is fixed at any one time and is the nominal unit value of one share times the number of shares allowed to be issued in accordance with MEMORANDUM AND ARTICLES OF ASSOCIATION.
- The number of shares issued at any one time is also fixed; the value of the issued share capital is the number of issued shares times he nominal value of one share. The issued share capital can be and often is less than the nominal share capital.

Thus:

SHARE CAPITAL

	£
Nominal –	
10,000 shares of £1 each	10,000
Issued –	
5,000 share of £1 each	5,000

ORDINARY SHARE CAPITAL

Ordinary SHARES attract the full risks and benefits accruing from the business. Subject to the rights of any other class of share, shareholders owning such shares are entitled to all the PROFITS of the business but also accept all its LOSSES. If the company goes into LIQUIDATION they will only receive back their CAPITAL after all other DEBTS have been paid.

As well as receiving dividend income they may also benefit from an increase in SHARE VALUE.

NOTES TO THE ACCOUNTS
A LIMITED COMPANY has to prepare A SET OF ACCOUNTS that provides certain information required by law. This can be substantial and to include it all in the PROFIT AND LOSS ACCOUNT and BALANCE SHEET would make them difficult to understand. Key information only is, therefore, usually included in the accounts and the rest in notes to the accounts.

Accounts for a partnership or sole trader may adopt the same principle, although there are few statutory requirements for information in such sets of accounts.

PARTNERSHIP

A partnership arises when two or more people go into business together but do not form a LIMITED COMPANY. The fundamental distinction is that they are the business and not separate from it. Accordingly, the partners, unlike shareholders, are respon- sible INDIVIDUALLY and TOGETHER for ALL the debts of the business. Their liability to pay the debts is unlimited and they can be required to sell personal assets to pay the LIABILITIES of the business.

The terms of the partnership are agreed between the partners and written in a partnership agreement which is the equivalent of a limited company's MEMORANDUM AND ARTICLES OF ASSOCIATION. Amongst other things it lays out how the profits and losses of the partnership are to be shared.

PAYMENT

An amount paid in cash or by a cheque – a CREDIT entry in a CASH BOOK. The DEBIT entry will be to a COST or CREDITOR ACCOUNT,

POSTING

An accounting term for recording a FINANCIAL TRANSACTION in an ACCOUNT.

PREPAYMENT

A type of DEBTOR, it is an amount paid in advance of the ACCOUNTING PERIOD to which it relates:

- A business makes up its accounts to 31st March and makes a payment for 6 months rent of £1200 on the 1st November (i.e. at £200 for each month from November to April). A prepayment exists at the 31st March of £200 – Aprils rent.
- If the business were to go into LIQUIDATION at the 31st March , all other things being equal, it would be owed the rent paid for April.

It is the opposite of an ACCRUAL, and is entered in the GENERAL JOURNAL before being POSTED to the GENERAL LEDGER

PREFERENCE SHARE CAPITAL

The preference shareholders share in the success of the business to a limited extent only, in return for a share of the profits in advance of the owners of ORDINARY SHARE CAPITAL.

Normally their income benefit is in the form of a fixed income per share given in percentage terms; for example, a business with a CAPITAL structure including 5% Preference Shares with a NOMINAL VALUE of

£1 pays 5p for each preference share issued, however great the profits of the business.

Preference shares do not normally attract any substantial increase in SHARE VALUE but preference shareholders receive repayment of their CAPITAL in LIQUIDATION before the ORDINARY SHAREHOLDERS.

There are different types of preference shares:

- Cumulative – If the company's profits are insufficient to pay the preference dividend in one year arrears are paid in the subsequent year(s) before any dividends are paid to ordinary shareholders
- Non-cumulative – any arrears of dividend payments are 'lost' if not paid
- Redeemable – the capital may be repaid to the preference shareholders at some future point in time
- Convertible – preference shares that may be transferred into some other class of share, normally ordinary shares, at some future point in time

Finally, preference shares may be a combination of the above variations. The rights and obligations are given in the company's MEMORANDUM AND ARTICLES OF ASSOCIATION.

PROFIT

A profit arises when all INCOMES related to a particular event or ACCOUNTING PERIOD are greater than the EXPENSES for that event or period. Thus a profit may arise from trading over a period of time or from the disposal of a FIXED ASSET.

Accumulated profits are the total of profits, less LOSSES, for a number of ACCOUNTING PERIODS, usually financial years; the accumulated profits on the BALANCE SHEET represent the total net results of the business to date, after all PROVISIONS and RESERVES.

PROFIT AND LOSS ACCOUNT

A financial report that matches the EXPENSES and INCOMES to the accounting period to which they relate rather than when the related payment is made or the receipt received. (See CONVENTIONS, matching).

It shows only the trading totals for a period, (e.g. **FROM** 1st January **TO** 31st December), without any major analysis, and a common presentation is as follows:

	£	£
SALES		x
LESS DIRECT EXPENSES		
Materials and parts	x	
Labour	x	(x)
GROSS PROFIT (LOSS)		x
LESS INDIRECT EXPENSES		(x)
PROFIT BEFORE DRAWINGS		x
DRAWINGS		(x)
PROFIT LOSS FOR THE PERIOD		x

INDIRECT EXPENSES are not normally allocated to product and services in a profit and loss account. (See EXPENSE ALLOCATIONS).

A SET OF ACCOUNTS invariably has to provide additional information, usually by way of NOTES TO THE ACCOUNTS

PROVISIONS

Amount set aside out of PROFITS for a particular purpose, for example as:

- DEPRECIATION provision, to purchase replacement assets and charge an ACCOUNTING PERIOD with the cost of a FIXED ASSET for that period
- Bad debt provision to provide for DEBTORS who may not pay their debts
- STOCK provision to reduce the cost of stock to its realisable VALUE in cash, that is, what the business estimates it could sell it for

(See supplement 3).

PURCHASE

An EXPENSE involving the receipt of goods, where goods are delivered in an ACCOUNTING PERIOD but are not involved by the supplier before the CUT-OFF DATE a purchase reserve must be created to bring the expense and LIABILITY into the correct accounting period. This is similar to an ACCRUAL.

The term purchase is also used to denote the activity of buying.

RECEIPTS

An amount received in cash or by cheque – a DEBIT entry in a CASH BOOK. The CREDIT entry will be to an INCOME or DEBTOR account,

REPORTING FINANCIAL RESULTS

There are two basic forms of reporting financial results:

- The 'STATUTORY' presentation (even if not required by law other than for tax purposes – e.g. in a PARTNER-SHIP or in a SOLE TRADER'S business)
  The PROFIT AND LOSS ACCOUNT showing the results for a period of time; often called the historic accounts because they report past financial history – see CONVERNTIONS, historic cost
  The BALANCE SHEET showing the company's ASSETS AND LIABILITIES at a point in time
- MANAGEMENT REPORTING
  A range of analyses prepared from the basic financial and other records to assist managers in the business decision process. (See MANAGE-MENT ACCOUNTS)

RESERVES

Amount of net profits put aside for a 'rainy day' – sometimes known as revenue reserves. There is little distinction between accumulated PROFITS and revenue reserves. (See BALANCE SHEET).

They differ from PROVISIONS in that they are not usually for a particular purpose, being rather the 'left over's', whereas a provision is an amount of profit put aside for a specific purpose.

A Capital reserve can be created when a non-trading PROFIT arises, for example, when a freehold building appreciates in VALUE and is worth more than its net book value. (See DEPRECIATION).

RESPONSIBILITY FOR ACCOUNTS

The responsibility for the proper preparation of a STATUTORY SET OF ACCOUNTS lies ONLY with the directors of a LIMITED COMPANY, and not any agent employed to prepare them. In the case of a partnership or sole trader the responsibility lies with partners or owner.

SALES

The delivery of goods or provision of services. (See INCOME). A sales reserve is created at the end of an ACCOUNTING PERIOD for deliveries of goods and services that have

been provided before the CUT-OFF DATE but NOT invoiced to the customer.
(See PREPAYMENTS).

SET OF BOOKS
There is no definition of a set of books nor does the law talk in their terms; rather it talks in terms of records to report certain information (which the business could not do but for keeping financial records in a set of books!)

What records a business, therefore, keeps and how it keeps them is up to it as long as any legal requirements are complied with.

In general terms a set of books comprises the following:

Books of prime entry also known as **DAY BOOKS**	**LEDGERS**
sales day book expense day book cash (day) book payroll **GENERAL JOURNAL**	**GENERAL LEDGER** subsidiary ledgers **CREDITORS DEBTORS FIXED ASSETS EXPENSES**

FINANCIAL TRANSACTIONS are first entered in the DAY BOOKS and the individual entries POSTED to the subsidiary ledgers with totals POSTED to the CONTROL ACCOUNTS in the GENERAL LEDGER. (See SUPPLEMENT 2).

SET OF ACCOUNTS
The term is generally take to mean the STATUTORY ACCOUNTS presentation, even if not required by law – THE PROFIT AND LOSS ACCOUNTS and BALANCE SHEET – which may be prepared as often as required by the managers of the business. (See MANAGE - MENT ACCOUNTS).

In the case of a LIMITED COMPANY the proper preparation of the annual accounts required by law is the RESPONSIBILITY of the directors, even if they employ an external accountant to prepare them.

A SHARE
Evidence of ownership in a LIMITED COMPANY, in the form of a share certificate, which entitles the owner, shareholder, to that share's proportion of the company's worth, benefits and obligations as is represented by that share to the total number of shares issued, Thus, if a company has an issued SHARE CAPITAL of 10,000 shares and Mr A has one of those shares he owns one ten-thousandth of the company, whatever that is worth and of is profits or losses. (See SHARE VALUE).

SHARE ASSET VALUE
One of three key values of a SHARE in a LIMITED COMPANY and calculated by dividing the number of shares issued into the financial VALUE of the NET ASSETS of the company. (See NOMINAL SHARE CAPITAL).

	£	£
FIXED ASSETS	**10,000**	
CURRENT ASSETS	**8,000**	
less **CURRENT LIABILITIES**	**(3,000)**	
NET CURRENT ASSETS		**5,000**
NET ASSETS		**15,000**
SHARE CAPITAL		
5,000 shares £1 nominal value	**5,000**	
Accumulated PROFITS	**10,000**	**15,000**

SHARE ASSET VALUE: £3

SHARE VALUE

This share valuThe share value normally has little direct relationship to the NOMINAL VALUE of a SHARE and is more related to its SHARE ASSET VALUE or to the 'worth' of a share in the eyes of a purchaser. The value of a share quoted on a stock exchange is governed at any one time simply AND ONLY by the supply of the shares in that company being offered for sale by shareholders wishing to sell and the demand by purchasers for that company's shares. If demand (purchasers) is greater than supply (sellers) the price will go up; if weaker the price will go down.

Thus, factors such as profitability, the general economy or the sector in which the company operates, rumours of a take-over, and many, many other factors, all influence the decision to buy or sell shares and thus its value.

In the case of a company not quoted on a stock exchange the shares are valued by a professional advisor according to certain criteria, including profit potential and GOODWILL.

- The NOMINAL value   £1
  The basic unit amount of a share, paid (subscribed) by an investor

- The SHARE ASSET value £3
  The net assets divided by the number of issued shares

- The market value   any value

SOLE TRADER

Effectively this is a 'PARTNERSHIP' of one. He or she is the business, takes all the PROFITS, beards all the LOSES and is responsible for all the LIABILITIES.

STATUTORY ACCOUNTING, STATUTORY ACCOUNTS, STATUTORY REPORTING

The term 'statutory' means in accordance with the law and normally applies only to LIMITED COMPANIES, which can have considerable reporting obligations placed on them to report to their shareholders. Small and very small companies have reporting dispensations.

The fundamental elements are a DIRECTORS' REPORT, a PROFIT AND LOSS ACCOUNT for a period of time past, in most cases a year, a BALANCE SHEET at a particular date and NOTES TO THE ACCOUNTS providing additional information needed to understand the accounts.

There is no 'statutory' requirement placed upon SOLE TRADERS and PARTNERSHIPS to produce a set of accounts although most certainly do, if only because they form the basis of agreeing the annual taxes to be paid.

Notwithstanding the requirement to report financial results, records have to be kept to account for Pay As You Earn, Value Added Tax, National Insurance Contributions and Corporation Tax.

The standard presentations look at what has happened in the past; they report actual results and they are sometimes therefore known as historic accounts. (See CONVENTIONS, historic accounts).

STOCK

Stocks are held for trading and are PURCHASES of materials and goods which the business ids going to sell wither by themselves as is, or as part of something else or after it has done something to them – (see WORK-IN-PROGRESS). Commonly, stocks include parts, raw materials and finished goods. They are in effect unused or unsold purchases at the CUT-OFF DATE and are carried forward for use in the following ACCOUNTING PERIOD.

The term can also be used in the sense of 'store' – a stock of stationery, stamps, fuel oil to feed the boilers. Often, but not always, there are included on the BALANCE SHEET as a PREPAYMENT. Alternatively, they may be treated as an EXPENSE to the PROFIT AND LOSS ACCOUNT if not material. (See CONVENTIONS, materiality).

TRIAL BALANCE

The fundamental rule of DOUBLE ENTRY ACCOUNTING is that every DEBIT entry MUST have its corresponding CREDIT entry and vice versa. Thus, as a BALANCE is the difference between the DEBITS and CREDITS on an ACCOUNT it follows that the total of the debit balances must equal the total of the credit balances.

The trial balance is a summary of the ACCOUNTING BALANCES in the GENERAL LEDGER and can be prepared at any time to prove mathematically that all entries have been made.

It does NOT prove that all entries have been POSTED to the CORRECT ACCOUNTS, only that all the debit entries equal all the credit entries. Mistakes in posting may have taken place or a FINANCIAL TRANSACTION incorrectly coded. (See SUPPLEMENT 2)

VALUE

FINANCIAL TRANSACTIONS that give rise to the ASSETS and LIABILITIES that appear on the BALANCE SHEET will have been initially POSTED in the LEDGERS at the amount of the original transaction.

However this may not be what they are

worth because the business might not be able to realise (obtain) their balance sheet amount in cash. Two examples:

- Your business is owned £1000 by X LTD and includes the amount in DEBTORS on the balance sheet. X LTD then goes bust and cannot pay its debts – the asset included in your balance sheet at £1000 is now worth nothing – it has no value
- You own a shop selling women's dresses and can't sell a STOCK of a particular summer fashion by the end of the season; the cost of unsold stock is £2000. If the fashion is likely to be dead next year the stock is now worth little or nothing and its value should be adjusted to no more than the estimated sales value – say £300.

In both cases the amount in the balance sheet must be reduced to the expected amount that will be received by the business. The entries would be:

	£	£
Dr PROFIT and LOSS ACCOUNT	1,000	
Cr DEBTORS		1,000
Dr PROFIT and LOSS ACCOUNT	1,700	
		1,700
Cr STOCK		

The effect is to reduce profits by the amount of the actual or expected loss to the business and reduce the value of the assets on the balance sheet to what they are worth – expected to realise in cash. (See CONVENTIONS, prudence). The above entries would be made by general entry in the GENERAL JOURNAL being adjustments rather than prime entries entered in a DAY BOOK.

The balance sheet should reflect the actual or estimated value of the business's assets and liabilities. DEPRECIATION is another example of 'writing down' an asset's COST to its estimated value. (See also SHARE ASSET VALUE).

WORK-IN-PROGRESS – WIP

If the business is one of manufacture, construction or processing there will be periods of time whilst the goods are manufactured, constructed or processed. STOCKS and OTHER DIRECT EXPENSES will be involved and the final result will be a product for SALE.

All the direct expenses involved to the point that the product or process is finished and ready for sale is known as work-in-progress. When in final product form it changes its nature and name to finished goods and if unsold at the end of an ACCOUNTING PERIOD is a stock of finished goods shown on the BALANCE SHEET.

Supplement 1

EXAMPLES OF DOUBLE ENTRY

I now give a number of examples of DOUBLE ENTRY ACCOUNTING to give a feel for what it is all about. Remember, the FINANCIAL TRANSACTIONS are presented as from the BUSINESS'S VIEWPOINT which is not the same as yours.

I open a bank account and pay in £5000:

	£	£
Dr CASH BOOK account	5000	
Cr CAPITAL account		5000

The business has an ASSET – cash in the form of a DEBIT owed by the bank – but also owes the amount to me, so it also has a LIABILITY.

I spend £1000 on buying some STOCK of special glassware from abroad:

	£	£
Dr STOCK account	1000	
Cr Cash Book account		1000

One asset goes up – stock – one goes down – cash.

I now sell £500 of stock for a SALES transaction of £800, for cash:

	£	£
Dr Cash Book account	800	
Cr SALES account		800

The following JOURNAL entries would be required to transfer the BALANCES on INCOME and EXPENDITURE accounts to the PROFIT AND LOSS ACCOUNT to establish the real outcome of trading:

	£	£
Dr Profit & Loss account	500	
Cr Stock account		500

and

	£	£
Dr Sales account	800	
Cr Profit & Loss account		800

The 'P & L' would then show a CREDIT BALANCE of £300, a profit, being the sale of £800 less the cost of sale £500.

I sell another £350 of stock for £600, but on credit, and get paid a month later. Of the remainder of the stock £100 is broken! And can be sold. The balance remains unsold.

The entries are:

	£	£
Dr DEBTORS account	600	
Cr Sales account		600

and when paid

	£	£
Dr Cash Book account	600	
Cr Debtors account		600

and the CLOSURE OF THE ACCOUNTS

	£	£
Dr Sales a/c	600	
Cr P & L a/c		600
Dr P & L a/c	350	
Cr Stock a/c		350
Dr P & L a/c	100	
Cr Stock a/c		100

The last entry above reduces the stock account for the breakage – it's a LOSS to the business, reducing profits.

After all the transactions have been entered the ACCOUNTS will look like this:

CASH

	Debit		Credit
	£		£
Cash paid in	5000	Stock purchased	1000
Cash sales	800	Balance	5400
Cash from Debtors	600		
	6400		6400

CAPITAL

	Debit		Credit
	£		£
Balance	5000	Cash paid in	5000

STOCK

	Debit		Credit
	£		£
Purchases	1000	Stock sold or	
		broken, to P & L a/c	950
		Balance	50
	1000		1000

SALES

	Debit		Credit
	£		£
Transfer to P & L a/c	1400	Cash Book	800
		Debtors	600
	1400		1400

DEBTORS

	Debit		Credit
	£		£
Sales	600	Cash Book	600

Now look at the entries below and determine what was actually happening in reality; the answers are on the next page.

		£	£
A	Dr Vehicle's a/c	750	
	Cr Creditors s/c		750
B	Dr Debtors a/c	75	
	Cr Sales a/c		75
C	Dr Creditors a/c	600	
	Cr Cash a/c		600
D	Dr Creditors a/c	50	
	Cr Stock a/c		50
E	Dr P & L a/c	100	
	Cr Provision for Depreciation a/c		100
F	Dr Cash a/c	80	
	Cr Debtors		80
G	Dr Rent a/c	400	
	Cr Accruals a/c		400
H	Dr P & L a/c	250	
	Cr Provision for bad debts a/c		250
I	Dr Cash a/c	90	
	Cr Bank interest a/c		90
J	Dr Provision for bad debts a/c	60	
	Cr Debtors a/c		60
K	Dr Debtors a/c	500	
	Cr Sales a/c		400
	Cr VAT a/c		100
L	Dr Wages a/c	290	
	Cr Cash a/c		200
	Cr PAYE a/c		90

And a few from a different angle . . . .

M What is the entry needed to pay the VAT in K above to the Customs and Excise?

N What entries are required to buy stationery of £60 on credit and then return half of it?

O Close off the sales account with a balance of £5000 at the end of the accounting period and a purchases account with a balance of £4000

P Open an account called 'Disposal of Fixed Assets Account', create the entries and determine what the profit or loss is on disposal for the following transactions: original cost of asset £1000; accumulated depreciation £900; proceeds on disposal £150.

A A vehicle was bought for £750 on credit

B Sales were made on credit

C A payment was made to a creditor

D Goods were returned from stock to the supplier

E A depreciation charge was created

F A debtor paid up

G An accrual was set up for rent

H Some profit was set aside to allow for debts that might not be paid

I Bank interest is credited to the bank account

J Some of the provision was used to absorb the loss arising when a debt went bad

K A sale was made on credit which included an amount for VAT which is owed to Customs and Excise, a liability

L The total wages cost was £290 of which £200 was paid to employees and a PAYE creditor set up for £90 to be paid later

		£	£
M	Dr VAT a/c	100	
	Cr Cash Book a/c		100
N	Dr Stationery a/c	60	
	Cr Creditors /c		60
	Dr Creditors a/c	30	
	Cr Stationery a/c		30
O	Dr Sales a/c	5000	
	Cr P & L a/c		4000
	Dr P & L a/c	4000	
	Cr Purchases a/c		4000
P	Dr Disposal of Fixed Asset a/c	1000	
	Cr Fixed Asset a/c		1000
	Dr Provision for Depreciation a/c	900	
	Cr Dr Disposal of Fixed Asset a/c		900
	Dr Cash a/c	150	
	Cr Disposal of Fixed Asset a/c		150
	Dr Disposal of Fixed Asset a/c	50	
	Cr P & L a/c		50

The last entry transfers the profit on disposal on the profit and loss account, and this might seem to be a non-trading profit which should not be credited to the P & L a/c.

You will see after brief reflection that the profit has arisen because too much depreciation have been charged over time to the P & L a/c, reducing the asset's 'net book value' to below what the asset could be sold for. Therefore, if the correct amount of depreciation could have been foreseen when the charges were originally made no profit would have arisen. The P & L a/c's in the past have, therefore, been charged with too much expense and the profit on disposal should now be credited to it.

Supplement 2

A PICTORIAL SUMMARY OF A SET OF FINANCIAL BOOKS AND REPORTS

Business decisions result in FINANCIAL TRANSACTIONS (A) – INCOMES and COSTS, PAYMENTS and RECEIPTS.

Financial transactions are entered in the DAY BOOKS and GENERAL JOURNAL (B).

The details are POSTED in the subsidiary ledgers © and totals posted to the GENERAL LEDGER (D).

At the ends of the ACCOUNTING PERIOD adjusting entries are made by journal entry, the ACCOUNTS are CLOSED OFF and the TRIAL BALANCE (E) prepared. The PROFIT AND LOSS ACCOUNT and BALANCE SHEET (F) are then drawn up.

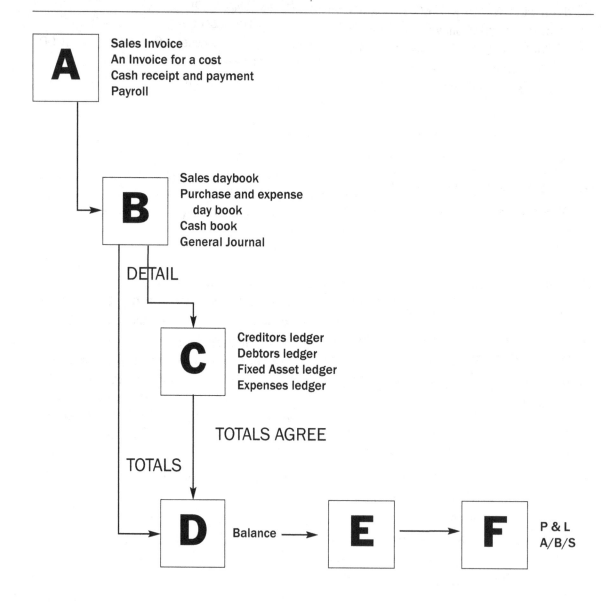

A
Sales Invoice
An Invoice for a cost
Cash receipt and payment
Payroll

B
Sales daybook
Purchase and expense
  day book
Cash book
General Journal

DETAIL

C
Creditors ledger
Debtors ledger
Fixed Asset ledger
Expenses ledger

TOTALS AGREE

TOTALS

D Balance →

E →

F P & L
A/B/S

Supplement 3

PROFIT IS CASH!

Consider the following balance sheet:

	£	£		£	£
SHAREHOLDER INTEREST			**FIXED ASSETS**		
Share capital	5000		Cost	3000	
Accumulated Profit	2000		Depreciation	(1000)	
	A	7000		**C**	2000
CURRENT LIABILITIES			**CURRENT ASSETS**		
Creditors	3000		Stock & WIP	2000	
			Debtors	2000	
	B	3000	Bank	4000	
				D	8000
					10000

Mathematically, A is equal to C plus D minus B. In other words the shareholders' interests are equal to the net assets of the company.

If follows that if the assets were sold for cash and realised £10,000, the creditors could be paid the £3000 owing to them leaving £7000 in the bank to pay the shareholders, part of which is accumulated profits.

What has happened is that over time, the original capital has been used to purchase fixed assets and trade profitability, changing in nature to the assets and liabilities shown on the balance sheet.

When one reduces profits (puts profits aside) in the Profit and Loss Account by creating a provision (or reserve) one is in effect putting aside net assets for a particular purpose and not making them available for drawings or dividends.

To prove the point, consider the depreciation provision of £1000. IF the P & L a/c had not been charged with (reduced by) the £1000 accumulated profits would have been £3000, still represented by net assets realisable into cash. The business has in effect put aside £1000 worth of net assets (cash) towards the replacement of its fixed assets, in the form of provision for depreciation.

By doing this, the P & L a/c's have shown less profit available for drawings or dividends than would otherwise have been the case, thereby preserving the net assets (cash) in the business, and not making them available for 'distribution'.

Supplement 4

APPARENT ANOMALIES

Why profits and liabilities both credit are balances in a set of accounts?

Because the business has a liability to pay the balances – it owes the amounts. If it makes a profit it owes the owners that profit, its shareholders or partners. If it owes money for purchases it has a trade creditor.

Why is sale shown on the 'same side' as a liability? (Credit)

Because, if there were no other expenses at all that sale would in effect be a profit to the business (a P & L a/c with income but no expenses) and therefore owed to the owners.

Why does an expense appear on the 'same side' as an asset? (Debit)

Simply because it is a special form of debt, an asset (but never considered as such). If the bank pays a cheque of £100 on behalf of the business for stationery, and there are no other transactions, the P & L a/c shows a loss of £100. The business, however, is still owed the money by the owners to pay off the bank, thus the owners owe the business the cash needed to pay for its expenses.

Appendix 1
MYBIZ

The assumptions are just the sort you might expect of someone setting up a small haulage business although the types of income and expenses have been kept to a minimum so as not to obscure the principles.

Harry started a light haulage business on the 1st March 2009 and set his financial year end date as 31st December – he runs the business from home.

THE VAN

He bought a second hand van on the 31st March for £8,000 which he expected to have to replace in 3 years time (March 2012) – Harry thinks he will be able to sell it then for £800.

Vehicle insurance is £1,200 per annum, paid monthly from March.

The road fund tax expired on 31st May and £240 was paid in June for 6 months – it was renewed in November at the same cost.

Harry decided to 'put aside' £50 per month for repairs and maintenance and had to pay for a new tyre in September which cost £100 – this expense was set against the provision.

Believing the business was growing he bought a trailer for £2,700 on the 30th November – under the terms of the purchase Harry was given three months to pay for it.

Harry will sell it with the van but expects to receive nothing got it.

THE GARAGE

Harry has rented a small lock-up garage since 1st May, paying 6 months in advance and then quarterly in advance – the annual cost is £1,800.

TRADING INCOME

Harry was fortunate to pick up a contract for a year to run a delivery service on a set route each month starting in June; the annual contract value is $4,800 paid monthly, but 2 months in arrears.

He charges other customers at £1.30 per mile and the miles driven in 1993 were:

March	100	August	1100
April	400	Sept.	1200
May	700	October	1300
June	700	November	1200
July	600	December	800

DIRECT OPERATING EXPENSES

Direct operating expenses are given above under van and garage except for fuel and oil which is £45 per month for the annual contract and 12 pence per mile for other work.

Direct expenses are all paid in the month.

INDIRECT EXPENSES

Advertising in a trade magazine was paid in March for a year at a cost of £300.

The telephone bill is paid in arrears in the month following the quarter at £150 each quarter, with effect from 1st March.

There was a one-off financial fee for advice on setting up the business of £300 paid in May. There was a similar amount for the audit of the accounts but it was not paid until 1994.

Harry took delivery of and paid for £360 worth of stationery on 1st April 1993 which he will use evenly to the end of March 1994.

Incidentals amount to £50 each month, paid in the month.

Harry draws £500 per month from the business for personal purposes.

FUNDING ARRANGEMENTS

The bank advanced £3,600 on 1st March towards the purchases of the vehicle repayable over 36 months. The capital element (£3,600) is repayable in equal monthly amounts and the first year's interest of £360 is also paid in equal monthly amounts.

Harry paid in the balance of the purchases price of the van and a further £1,000 as capital.

The bank also allowed Harry an overdraft facility of £2,000, interest being calculated at a rate of 10% on the average of the opening and closing monthly balance, if negative, charged in the following month – similarly, interest of 4 % is paid on a positive balance, similarly calculated.

The cash flows of the business were such that Harry had to pay further amounts of capital into the business in June & July totalling £700, £400 in June and £300 in July.

❋ ❋ ❋ ❋ ❋ ❋ ❋ ❋

Prepare the:
- Cash Flow Report
- Double entry accounts and trial balance
- Profit and Loss Account and Balance Sheet

❋ ❋ ❋ ❋ ❋ ❋ ❋ ❋

To help you with the cash flow reports go through the following steps:
- Obtain four or five sheets of lined and columned paper
- Enter the months March to December along the top of the page with a total column for the ten months to December on the right hand side
- Enter the descriptions of the receipts and payments down the left hand side
- Group like receipts and payments together under the following headings:

  Direct trading expenses

  Indirect expenses

  Capital fixed assets

  Start-up payments

  Funding

Produce sub-totals for each group and then one grant total at the foot of the page of the sub-totals
- Calculate the balance at the end of each month and take it forward to the beginning of the following month
- Enter the receipts and payments from the assumptions

If you like, have a quick look at the layout of our answers on the next page to give you an impression of how it looks.

❋ ❋ ❋ ❋ ❋ ❋ ❋ ❋

THE FINANCIAL STATEMENTS

Statement of CASH FLOW and PROFIT AND LOSS ACCOUNT for the 10 months to 31st December 2009 and BALANCE SHEET as at that date:

STATEMENT OF CASH FLOW

JANUARY to JUNE	Ref	Jan	Feb	Mar	Qtr Total	Apr	May	June	Qtr Total
Fee paying miles driven				100		400	700	800	
at £1.30 per mile		£	£	£	£	£	£	£	£
Trading Receipts	A								
Set Contract		0	0	0	0	0	0	0	0
Casual Business		0	0	130	130	520	910	780	2210
Less		0	0	130	130	520	910	780	2210
Trading payments, cost of	B								
sales - see analysis		0	0	-112	-112	-148	-1084	-457	-1689
Gross trading cash position	C=A-B	0	0	18	18	372	-174	323	521
Less	D								
Trading payments									
Overheads									
Telephone		0	0	0	0	0	0	-150	-150
Incidentals		0	0	-50	-50	-50	-50	-50	-150
	E=C-D	0	0	-32	-32	322	-224	123	221
Less									
Drawings to owner	F	0	0	-500	-500	-500	-500	-500	-1500
Net trading cash position	G=E-F	0	0	-532	-532	-178	-724	-377	-1279
Less									
Capital Costs	H	0	0	0	0	0	0	0	0
		0	0	-532	-532	-178	-724	-37	-1279
Less									
Start-up payments	J								
Capital					0				0
Van				-8000	-8000				0
Revenue									
Advertising				-300	-300				0
Accounting Fee					0		-300		-300
Stationery					0	-360			-360
	K=I-J	0	0	-8832	-8832	-538	-1024	-377	-1939
Funding arrangements	L								
Capital paid in: Harry				5400	5400			400	400
Loans paid in: Bank				3600	3600				0
Capital repaid									
Loans repaid: Bank									
Capital				-100	-100	-100	-100	-100	-300
Interest				-30	-30	-30	-30	-30	-90
Interest on the bank account		0	0	0	0	1	-21	-60	-80
Full cash flow, in the month		0	0	38	38	-667	-1175	-167	-2009
Balance Calculation									
Opening Balance		0	0	0	0	38	-629	-1804	38
In the month cash flow	M	0	0	38	38	167	-1175	-167	-2009
CLOSING BALANCE		**0**	**0**	**38**	**38**	**-629**	**804**	**1971**	**-1971**

JULY to DECEMBER	Ref	Jul	Aug	Sept	Qtr Total	Oct	Nov	Dec	Qtr Total	Annual Total
Fee paying miles driven		500	1100	1200		1300	1200	800		
at £1.30 per mil		£	£	£	£	£	£	£		£
Trading Receipts	A									
Set Contract		0	400	400	800	400	400	400	1200	2000
Casual Business		650	1430	1560	3640	1690	1560	1040	4290	
10270										
Less		650	1830	1960	4440	2090	1960	1440	5490	
12270										
Trading payments, cost of sales - see analysis	B	-205	-277	-389	-871	-301	-739	-481	-1521	-4193
Gross trading cash position	C=A-B	445	1553	1571	3569	1789	1221	959	3969	8077
Less										
Trading payments	D									
Overheads										
Telephone		0	0	-150	-150	0	0	-150	-150	-450
Incidentals		-50	-50	-50	-150	-50	-50	-50	-150	-500
	E=C-D	395	1503	1371	3269	1739	1171	759	3669	7217
Less										
Drawings to owner	F	-500	-500	-500	-1500	-500	-500	-500	-1500	-5000
Net trading cash position	G=E-F	-105	1003	871	1769	1239	671	259	2169	2127
Less										
Capital Costs	H	0	0	0	0	0	0	0	0	0
		-105	1003	871	1769	1239	671	259	2169	2127
Less										
Start-up payments	J									
Capital					0				0	0
Van					0				0	-8000
Revenue										
Advertising					0				0	-300
Accounting Fee					0				0	-300
Stationery					0				0	-360
K=I-J	-105	1003	871	1769	1239	671	259	2169	-6833	
Funding arrangements	L									
Capital paid in: Harry		300			300				0	6100
Loans paid in: Bank										
Capital repaid										
Loans repaid: Bank										
Capital		-100	-100	-100	-300	-100	-100	-100	-300	-1000
Interest		-30	-30	-30	-90	-30	-30	-30	-90	-300
Interest on the bank account		-66	-66	-39	-170	-15	21	20	25	-225
Full cash flow, in the month	M=K+/-L	-1	807	702	1509	1094	562	149	1804	1342
Balance Calculation										
Opening Balance		-1971	-1972	-1165	-1971	-463	631	1193	-463	0
In the month cash flow	M	-1	807	702	1509	1094	562	149	1804	1342
CLOSING BALANCE		1972	1165	-463	-463	631	1193	1342	1342	1342

ANALYSIS

JANUARY to JUNE	Ref	Jan	Feb	Mar	Qtr Total	Apr	May	June	Qtr Total
		£	£	£	£	£	£	£	£
Trading payments	B								
Insurance		0	0	-100	-100	-100	-100	-100	-300
Road fund tax		0	0	0	0	0	0	-240	-240
Replacement tyre		0	0	0	0	0	0	0	0
Garage		0	0	0	0	0	-900	0	-900
Fuel - annual contract		0	0	0	0	0	0	-45	-45
Fuel - casual business		0	0	-12	-12	-48	-84	-72	-204
		0	**0**	**-112**	**-112**	**-148**	**-1084**	**-457**	**-1689**

JULY to DECEMBER	Ref	Jul	Aug	Sept	Qtr Total	Oct	Nov	Dec	Qtr Total	Annual Total
		£	£	£	£	£	£	£		£
Trading payments	B									
Insurance		-100	-100	-100	-300	-100	-100	-100	-300	-1000
Road fund tax		0	0	0	0	0	0	-240	-240	-480
Replacement tyre		0	0	-100	-100	0	0	0	0	-100
Garage		0	0	0	0	0	-450	0	-450	-1360
Fuel - annual contract		-45	-45	-45	-135	-45	-45	-45	-135	-315
Fuel - casual business		-60	-132	-144	-336	-156	-144	-96	-396	-940
		-205	**-277**	**-389**	**-871**	**-301**	**-739**	**-481**	**-1521**	**-4193**

Please ignore rounding differences

NOTES TO THE CASH FLOW REPORT

Remember that the cash flow statements place the receipt or payments in the month it is received or paid and NOT the month to which the transaction relates. Thus, if you pay 3 months rent on the 31st December, in advance, the cash is paid in December but it is the true expense of the following three months.Also note:

- That the cash flow is presented in a layout to help a bank, starting with the trading cash position (C, E, G), moving into capital expenditure and start-up requirements (H,J) and finally the initial funding requirements (L). It is laid out in this manner because the nature of financing may be different for each group of transactions – trading on overdraft, capital fixed assets on loan or lease, funding on loan or overdraft – and it will help the bank to decide which is most appropriate in the circumstances

- We regard the information we show in the Analysis as detail and the totals were taken to the main part of the report. It would have been equally correct however to enter all items on the main statement if that is what you want

- Although it is unlikely that your layout is exactly the same as ours the answer should, nevertheless, be the same

Now have a go at preparing the double entry accounts – the 'T' accounts.

✻ ✻ ✻ ✻ ✻ ✻ ✻ ✻ ✻

DOUBLE ENTRY ACCOUNTING

Before you start REMEMBER . . .

- The entries are made from the BUSINESS' viewpoint NOT Harry's
- Each type of transaction has its own account
- There are two sides to each account – debit on the left and credit on the right:

ACCOUNT NAME

DEBITS £	CREDITS £
Things belonging to the business - vehicles, buildings, plant furniture and fittings, positive bank balances, stock Amounts owed to the business - debts, prepayments Expenses	Amounts owed by the business - to creditors, loans, capital paid to the business Profit - Owed by the business to the owners Income - sale

- A BALANCE is the difference between the total on one side of an account and the other
- Transactions are recorded twice:
  Once as to how it affects the inside of the business
  The cost and income accounts
  Once on how it affects the outside of the business
  the bank, creditors, debtors and Harry are outside the business
- Consider now the cash flow statements; the difference between the receipts and payments for the 10 months was a positive difference of £1342. The double entry account called BANK (cash book) shows all those transactions in the following way:
  All the amounts Harry has paid out are owed TO the bank; all the amounts that Harry has paid in to the account are owed BY the bank

to Harry. The difference, BALANCE, is the net amount the bank owes Harry – in this case the receipts (the amount paid into the bank Harry owed by it to him) are greater than the amounts he owes the bank in the form of payments

Every entry in the bank account has to be recorded elsewhere, thus insurance and fuel and rent have their own account where the 'other half' of the bank account entries are recorded; thus the total of insurance and fuel and tent are also established

To set you on your way:

- Prepare some 30 bank 'T' accounts in which to enter your transactions
  Prepare your entries by taking the TOTALS for each item for the ten months from the cash flow report. You should use our report for the next part of the exercise if you want

- to check your set of accounts against ours
- Open the Cash Book as you first 'T' account in which to enter the RECEIPTS and PAYMENTS
- As you open an account name it and make the entries. MAKE BOTH ENTRIES AT THE SAME TIME – THE CREDIT AND THE DEBIT – SO AS NOT TO FORGET ONE! REMEMBER THAT EVERY DEBIT ENTRY MUST HAVE A CREDIT ENTRY OTHERWISE THE TRIAL BALANCE WILL NOT BALANCE
- When you have entered all the transactions from the receipts and payments go bank through the assumptions and prepare the adjustments for NON-CASH TIMES – Depreciation, accruals and prepayments, sales reserves and creditors at the cut off date
- Ignore day books and journal entries, entering all prime entries and adjustments direct in the accounts to which they relate
- When ALL entries have been made calculate the balance on each account and prepare the Trial Balance

Again, have a quick look at the layout of the answer to get a picture of how to present the 'T' accounts. The 'T' accounts are in no particular order simply that in which we opened them. In practice, accounts in the general ledger are grouped by their nature, for example all fixed assets together, all stock and work-in-progress together, all income together, and so on.

✽ ✽ ✽ ✽ ✽ ✽ ✽ ✽ ✽

'T' ACCOUNTS PRESENTING
THE DOUBLE ENTRY ACCOUNTING OF HARRY'S BUSINESS

Note: the dates in certain cases are abbreviated, e.g. M/D Insurance, £1000 means the payments from March to December

CASH BOOK

		£			£
M/D	Sales	10270	Mar	Van	8000
Mar	Loans	3600	Mar	Advertising	300
Mar	Harry, Capital	5400	M/D	Insurance	1000
J/D	Bank interest	42	M/D	Fuel, casual	948
June	Harry, Capital	400	M/D	Incidentals	500
July	Harry, capital	300	M/D	Drawings	5000
A/D	Sales	2000	M/D	Loan repayment	1000
			M/D	Loan interest	300
			M/D	Bank a/c, interest	267
			Apr	Stationery	360
			May	Rent	900
			May	Financial Fee	300
			June	Road Refund Tax	240
			J/D	Fuel, contract	315
			J/D	Telephone	450
			Sept	Tyre	100
			Nov	Rent	450
			Dec	Road Fund Tax	240
			31 Dec	Balance	1342
		22012			**22012**

VEHICLES

		£			£
Mar	Bank (Van	8000			
Nov	Creditor (Trailer)	2700	31 Dec Balance		10700
		10700			**10700**

INSURANCE

		£			£
Mar	Bank	1000	31 Dec Balance		10000
		1000			**1000**

ROAD FUND TAX

	£		£
June Bank	240	31 Dec Prepayment	200
Dec Bank	240	31 Dec Balance	280
	480		**480**

GARAGE RENT

	£		£
May Bank	900	31 Dec Prepayment	90
Nov Bank	450	31 Dec Balance	1260
	1360		**1360**

SALES

	£		£
		M/D Bank, Casual	10270
		31 Dec Bank, Contract	2000
31 Dec Balance	13070	31 Dec Debtor, Contract	800
	13070		**13070**

PREPAYMENTS

	£		£
31 Dec Rent	90		
31 Dec Road Fund tax	200		
31 Dec Advertising	60	31 Dec Balance	440
31 Dec Stationery	90		
	440		**440**

PROVISION FOR REPAIRS

	£		£
Sep Bank (Tyre)	90	M/D Charge	500
31 Dec Balance	200		
	290		**290**

PROVISION CHARGE

	£		£
M/D Provision	500	31 Dec Balance	500
	500		**500**

CREDITORS

	£			£
		Nov Vehicles		2700
		31 Dec Telephone		50
31 Dec Balance	3050	31 Dec Audit		300
	3050			**3050**

DEBTORS

	£		£
31 Dec Sales, contract	800	31 Dec Balance	800
	800		**800**

FUEL

	£		£
J/D Bank contract	315		
M/D Bank, casual	948	31 Dec Balance	1263
	1263		**1263**

ADVERTISING

	£		£
Mar Bank	300	31 Dec Prepayments	60
		31 Dec Balance	240
	300		**300**

TELEPHONE

	£		£
J/D Bank	450		
31 Dec Creditors	50	31 Dec Balance	500
	500		**500**

FINANCIAL AND AUDIT

	£		£
May Bank, Financial Fee	300		
31 Dec Creditors, audit	300	31 Dec Balance	600
	600		**600**

STATIONERY

	£		£
Apr Bank	360	31 Dec Prepayments	90
		31 Dec Balance	270
	360		360

INCIDENTALS

	£		£
M/D Bank	500	31 Dec Balance	500
	500		500

DRAWINGS

	£		£
M/D Bank	5000	31 Dec Balance	5000
	360		360

BANK LOAN

	£		£
M/D Bank, repayments	1000	Mar Bank	3600
31 Dec Balance	2600		
	3600		3600

HARRY'S CAPITAL

	£		£
		Mar Bank	5400
		June Bank	400
31 Dec Balance	6100	July Bank	300
	6100		6100

LOAN INTEREST

	£		£
M/D Bank	300	31 Dec Balance	300
	300		300

BANK ACCOUNT INTEREST

	£		£
J/D Bank, overdraft	267	J/D Bank a/c interest	42
		31 Dec Balance	225
	267		267

DEPRECIATION PROVISION

	£		£
		31 Dec Depreciation charge	
		- Van	2000
		- Trailer	100
	2100		**2100**

DEPRECIATION CHARGE

	£		£
31 Dec Provision			
- Van	2000		
- Trailer	100	31 Dec Balance	2100
	2100		**2100**

ADJUSTMENTS

We have stressed that the difference between a cash flow and a profit report and a profit report is that the former presents the cash transactions when they take place and the latter in the time period to which the transactions relate. This will become clearer as we explain some of the adjustments we have made no prepare the Profit and Loss Account and Balance Sheet – remember that the accounts are for the 10 month period to 31st December.

- **The Trailer:** The business received it at the end of November buy did not pay for it until the next year. An entry must be made to increase VEHICLES and because it was not paid for by 31st December the amount is also entered in CREDITORS.

- **Other creditor adjustments** are for telephone and audit. In the first case the business will not pay for the December charge until March so it therefore has to 'accrue' an estimate for one month's expense.

The audit cost also relates to the period to December 1993 and must be similarly accrued.

- **Road fund tax** – in this case a payment is made at the beginning of December for 6 months; it would be wrong for the Profit and Loss Account to December to include the full amount so an adjustment is made to reduce the cost in the ROAD FUND TAX account and transfer the amount paid in respect of January to May 1994 to PREPAYMENTS account. A similar adjustment is made for rent, advertising and stationery.

- **Sales** – the cash receipts in respect of the contract work are in effect 2 months in arrears because Harry's business has allowed 2 months credit. This means that he is owed for the work done in November and December – he has a debtor for 2 months sales and a sales reserve adjustments is made to increase SALES and DEBTORS by £800.

- **Depreciation:** In principle this, too, is simply a 'timing' adjustment. The van cost £8000 and is expected to last 36 months so its cost must be spread over the accounting periods of the 36 months. In this case, however, Harry expects to sell the ban for £800 so the true cost to the business over the 36 months will be £8000 minus £800, £7,200 - £200 per month. So this period's accounts (March to December) should be 'charged' with 10 months use at £200 - £2000. A similar calculation is done for the trailer.

So how is this presented? One could simply reduce the amount of the VEHICLES' account by the amount by the amount of the depreciation, charging I to the Profit and Loss Account. If we did this, however, we would lost sight of the original cost so convention has it that when the adjustment is made two accounts are opened – one for the Charge to the Profit and Loss Account and the other to the Depreciation Provision Account.

- **The provision for repairs** – this operates in almost exactly the same way as the depreciation accounts. Once the provision is created it is used to bear the expense of repairs. If the expense of the tyre had been debited to P & L a/c and not the provision account, profit would have been reduced by a further £100 (or the loss similarly increased) and the provision would have remained unused at £500.

Now on to the 'TB'

✾ ✾ ✾ ✾ ✾ ✾ ✾ ✾ ✾

THE TRIAL BALANCE

Once all the entries have been made the balance is established for each account by determining the difference between the debit entries and credit entries. If the debits are greater an amount has to be entered **ON THE CREDIT SIDE** to bring the total of the two columns to equal each other.

Because two entries have been made for each transaction it is a truism that the total of all the debit balances must equal the total of the credit balances.

The **TRIAL BALANCE** is a summary of all the balances and the total of the debit column should be the same as the total of the credit column.

Now 'extract' all the balances and prepare the 'TB'

✾ ✾ ✾ ✾ ✾ ✾ ✾ ✾ ✾

MYBIZ
TRIAL BALANCE at 31 DECEMBER 2009

	Balances	
	Debit **£**	**Credit** **£**
Vehicles	10700	
Insurance	1000	
Road Fund Tax	280	
Garage Rent	1260	
Sales		13070
Bank	1342	
Prepayments	440	
Provision for repairs		400
Repairs provision charge	500	
Creditors		3050
Debtors	800	
Fuel	1263	
Advertising	240	
Telephone	500	
Financial and audit	600	
Stationery	270	
Incidentals	500	
Drawings	5000	
Bank loan		2600
Harry's capital		6100
Loan interest	300	
Bank account interest	225	
Depreciation provision		2100
Depreciation charge	2100	
	27320	**27320**

THE P & L A/C AND B/S

Prepare the P & L a/c by entering the income and expense accounts from the TB – this time refer to the layout in Part A, P & L a/c, and not the answer that follows!

When you have arrived at the result for the year prepare the B/S by entering the remaining balances – assets and liabilities and the result from the P & L a/c.

Now add the totals of both sides of the balance sheet and . . . ? (Are they the same?).

MYBIZ
PROFIT AND LOSS ACCOUNT FOR THE PERIOD
MARCH to DECEMBER 2009

	£	£	£
SALES			13070
Less **DIRECT EXPENSES:**			
Vehicle running expenses	1000		
- insurance	280		
- road and tax	1263	2543	
Other vehicle related expenses			
- garage rent	1260		
- vehicle depreciation	2100		
- provision for repairs	500	3860	(6403)
GROSS PROFIT			
INDIRECT EXPENSES			
- advertising	240		
- telephone	500		
- stationery	270		
- incidentals	500		
- financial and audit	600		
- loan interest	300		
- bank account interest	225		**(2635)**
PROFIT BEFORE DRAWINGS			**4032**
DRAWINGS			**(5000)**
ACCOUNTING LOSS FOR THE PERIOD			**(968)**

MYBIZ
BALANCE SHEET at 31st DECEMBER 2009

	£	£		£	£
HARRY			**FIXED ASSETS**		
Capital	6100		Cost of vehicles	10700	
Less loss	(968)	6132	Less depreciation	(2100)	8600
REPAIRS PROVISION	400				
LIABILITIES			**CURRENT ASSETS**		
Creditors	3050		Debtors	800	
Bank loan	2600	5650	Prepayments	440	
		11182	Bank balance	1342	2582
					11182

THE PROFIT AND LOSS ACCOUNT AND BALANCE SHEET

The Profit and Loss Account gives the result of TRADING – the income and expenses of trading THROUGH TIME. The BALANCE SHEET presents the NON-TRADING balances AT A POINT IN TIME – in this case the 31st December.

Again, how we have grouped the balances in the P & L Account is subjective but we think our presentation clearly brings out the relationship between vehicle-related and bib-vehicle related expenses.

Convention has it that ONLY in a balance sheet the debits are on the right and credits on the left!

COMMENTARY ON THE RESULTS

The key point to note is the difference in the results – cash (a positive balance of £1342) and loss (a negative result of £968). Which is right? They are both right. Which is more important? They are both important.

- The 'profit' result (in this case a loss) is the basic for calculating tax and has resulted because expenses exceeded income. Harry should not have taken so much out of the business in drawings!
- The cash result is positive – but for how long?

But they do relate to each other – cash to profit or loss. Harry's interest in the business has decreased in value because of the loss. In other words, if he were able to realise all his assets in cash for £11182 and pay off all his creditors of £5650 he would only be left with £5532, less than the amount of capital he originally put in to the business, another reason for not taking so much in drawings.

If Harry's business was a limited company he would not be allowed by law to reduce his original capital in this way. This business, therefore, is owed – has a debt – for the amount of the loss, an example of the third anomaly in Supplement 4. (See also SUPPLEMENT 3).

CONCLUSION

It may still be a clear as mud! But if points are not clear keep working at them. Double entry accounting can be confusing but only until the penny drops! . . . And it does!

The most important thing to remember is that all the entries and the resulting P & L a/c and B/S are prepared from the business' point of view – you are outside of it when considering the accounting. Once this is grasped all will fall into place and the more complicated aspects will be understood with comparative ease.

GOOD LUCK

Appendix H
GOLDEN RULES FOR BIDDING FOR WORK

- KNOW YOUR CUSTOMER
- UNDERSTAND THE COMPETITION
- MATCH THE PRODUCT YOU ARE OFFERING TO THE CUSTOMER'S NEEDS
- WRITE THE PROPOSAL DOCUMENT FROM THE CUSTOMER'S VIEWPOINT
- START EARLY

* * * * * * * * *

BE HONEST – IF THERE IS NO REASONABLE CHANCE OF WINNING DON'T BID

* * * * * * * * *

KNOW YOUR CUSTOMER

- Identify the customer as one or more individuals
- Is one or more the decision maker?
  Understand his real needs
  Understand his unexpressed needs
  Understand his priorities
- Understand how the customer will evaluate the proposal
  Who will evaluate it?
  What are their priorities?
- Have you bid to the customer before?
  What was the result and why?

UNDERSTAND THE COMPETITION

- Who are the competition
  What will the competition be offering?
  Why might the customer prefer the competition?
  What are their strengths and how can you negate them?

MATCH THE PRODUCT WE ARE OFFERING TO THE CUSTOMER'S NEEDS

- The customer will choose the supplier who can best meet his needs

WRITE THE PROPOSAL DOCUMENT FROM THE CUSTOMER'S VIEW POINT

- The customer will recognise the offer as the best if it is well written and focuses on his needs and priorities
- It should:
  Be clear, concise and easy to read
  Address all the issues that concern the customer and not the ones that worry you

START EARLY . . .

- In order to:
  Make the assessment to bid/not bid on good facts
  Give yourself time to ensure it is professional

Section Three

DO YOU HAVE THE SKILLS TO SUCCEED?

Contents
Section Three

Section Three
Do you have the skills to succeed?

INTRODUCTION

Considering starting up a business?

- Are you confused about where to start and the possible different approaches to start your own business?

- Are your reasons for starting a business a one-off? What are the most common reasons for other people going in business?

- Can you get good, practical advice on what to consider before going ahead?

- How can you research and develop your business idea?

- How can you develop your business idea into a viable, commercial product or service; particularly at this early critical stage when so much is unsure?

- What is a business plan? How do you prepare one? Why is it essential to create and use a business plan when starting a new business and in the first year?

- How can you improve your chances of survival until your business if off the ground?

- Personally speaking, how can you keep yourself afloat during the early months of your new business?

- When will you be ready to start up?

- Do you have what it takes to set up a new business?

- What are the common mistakes when starting up – and how do you avoid these mistakes?

Reducing the risks of an early business failure

Launching a small business is risky and although success can be very rewarding, business success can never be 100% guaranteed. Government statistics have shown that businesses are most vulnerable to failure duriing their early years of trading, with approximately 20 per cent of new businesses folding within their first year and 50 per cent within their first three years.

These figures should not scare you off, but should prepare you for some of the challenges you will face when starting your business. With hard work and an awareness of the issues, you can make sound plans and take decisions that will limit the possibilities of failure – and significantly improve your chances of long-term business success.

As examples, your chances of failure will increase significantly if you have:

- Been unrealistic – Set your costs too low or set your sights too high.

- Ignored, underestimated or not looked closely at the competition.

- Carried out poor or inadequate market research.

- Not done 'the sums' properly – leading to weak financial planning.

- Planned poorly – as examples, if you have not costed your products or services properly, or if you have poor stock and cost controls.

- Not thought through the business skills that you will need to have available in the business.

At this stage you may be unsure because there are so many questions to be answered and you may not really understand the questions let along be able to answer them.

The following checklist will help you to keep track of what you may need to learn during the time that you are planning and deciding your business. Review your existing business and your own personal strengths and weaknesses. Tick off the checklist as you learn the things that you need to and watch your progress and you confidence grow.

BUSINESS AWARENESS CHECKLIST

YOUR BUSINESS - things you may need to know	No idea 1	2	3	Could answer confidently 4
BUSINESS FOCUS				
● How to identify your business idea's unique selling point and why this will be successful.				
● If your business idea is worth developing or adapting.				
● What information is available on the overall needs of your business.				
BUSINESS INFRASTRUCTURE				
● What impact the organisation of your proposed business will have on;				
Who does what (for example, operations bookkeeping, sales calls, chasing up payment, etc.)				
The quality of customer service (for example, communications, billing, customer relation-ships).				
CASH FLOW				
● How to forecast business income and spending.				
● What funds will be spent when starting and/or running your business.				
● What the requirements are for forecasting cash flow				
● How to prepare and make sense of cash flow statements & forecasts.				
● How to monitor cash flow. (For example, by keeping day to day records and making sense of bank statements.)				
● How to choose the most useful timescales for financial forecasts. (E.g. every month, three months or a year.)				

YOUR BUSINESS - things you may need to know	No idea 1	2	3	Could answer confidently 4
• How to control sources and uses of cash. (For example, by moving cash between accounts, buying and selling stock, keeping the numbers of creditors and bad debtors to a minimum, managing payment to creditors, paying tax, buying and selling assets, and short-term sales and pricing policies.)				
• How the timing of cash receipts and spending affects cash flow.				
• How not meeting agreements can affect cash (E.g. not meeting delivery times, not following laws or breach of contract, non-acceptance of goods.)				
COMPETITORS				
• How your competitors will affect your business.				
• Where to find out about your competitors products or services.				
• How competitors' products or services may differ (for example price, quality, delivery times, payment terms, level of service).				
• How to analyse the market and competition.				
CONSULTATION				
• Why it is important to ask others for feedback and listen to what they say. (For example family, funders, stakeholders, customers)				
CUSTOMERS				
• How to build good relationships with customers (for example, responding to queries in a timely manner, being flexible and making the extra effort to meet their requirements).				
• How you can improve the experience your customers have when dealing with your business for example, by being available to them, tailoring products or services to meet their specific needs, etc).				

YOUR BUSINESS - things you may need to know	No idea 1	2	3	Could answer confidently 4
• How to regularly remind customers of the benefits of dealing with your business.				
• What feedback to get from customers (for example, why they choose to do business with you, how you can improve service and what new products or services you could offer).				
• Effective ways to get feedback from customers.				
• How to tell customers how you have used their feedback.				
FINANCES				
• How to research and estimate the costs of the main items of expenditure, such as premises, equipment, supplies and any staff you may need to employ.				
• How to estimate the cost of your market research.				
• How to work out the right price for your products or services.				
• How to work out your expenditure.				
• How to produce and use forecasts estimates and projections of finance for your business. (For example, cash flow forecasts, break-even, profit and loss, income and spending and budgets for specific areas like marketing.)				
• How to judge which information is reliable enough to base financial targets on.				
• How to set clear business and financial objectives that are realistic, achievable and can be measured.				
• How to identify different financial providers or potential funders (for example through directories, business advice services, through websites, trade journals, trade associations, venture capital associations, press, brokers, banks & accountants.)				

YOUR BUSINESS - things you may need to know	No idea 1	2	3	Could answer confidently 4
● How to choose the appropriate finance providers.				
● How to work out the cost of borrowing in terms of: Interest due, capital repayments, fees; and How the costs vary with any changes in the interest rates.				
● How your business financial needs should be presented to providers – and understanding what they may want in return from your business.				
● What security you might need to provide. The differences between secured and unsecured loans and the effect of making a personal guarantee.				
● How to agree terms and conditions.				
● What paperwork should be used for recording financial agreements?				
● Why it is frequently important to seek advice before signing contracts.				
● How to identify different needs of your business for finance. (for example, to set up the business, to keep the business trading (liquidity), profitability, receiving the most interest, keeping interest costs and borrowing charges down, paying for insurance and making sure that you have enough assets to meet the terms of finance.)				
● How to identify different types of financial help. (For example, secured loans, overdrafts, sale or lease back of assets, share ownership plans, insurance policies, use of pension funds, loan guarantee schemes, external funding for equity capital or debt financing and venture capital from business 'angels.')				

YOUR BUSINESS - things you may need to know	No idea 1	2	3	Could answer confidently 4
● How to work out:				
The costs of different kinds of finance (for example, interest charges, administration charges, fees, commission, equity and capital gain, insurance, penalties for early termination, penalties for failure to meet interest and principal repayments, security requirements and risk); and				
The benefits of different kinds of finance (for example, availability of funds, cash flow, investment and the effect on business).				
● What the likely risks to your business are and how these should be assessed. (For example risks that your business cannot repay an agreed loan and other debts, possible loss of control or even ownership of your business).				
● How to access the financial state of your business. (For example in terms of profit, cash flow, current assets and liabilities.)				
● How much profit you hope to make, how to cost your product or service and how to work out a selling price.				
● How to understand and use cash-flow forecasts and profit and loss accounts and what information you would need to produce them.				
LAW AND REGULATIONS				
● What laws will affect your business idea & how?				
● Which aspects of national and local law and regulations apply to your sort of business?				
● Which aspects of national and local law and regulations apply to all businesses, and to your own?				

YOUR BUSINESS - things you may need to know	No idea			Could answer confidently
	1	2	3	4

LEGAL FORMAT

- What the different types of legal status are that your business could have. (for example sole trader, partnership, limited company and industrial and providence societies.)

- What effect different options may have on your business in terms of customers and suppliers?

- Which type of trading status is best for meeting the commercial and other needs of your business?

SALES

- Why planning sales is important.

- Why setting targets for a sale is important.

- How to get targets for sales considering.
  Sales volume;
  Profit margins;
  Cash flow;
  Providing customer service;
  Getting repeat business;
  Product or service quality; and
  Weather clients are creditworthy.

- How to judge whether or not you are meeting sales targets

- How to include some flexibility in judging success, to take account of what actually happens.

- How to set up your business to make sure that you can get information about sales easily.

- How to identify the points at which your results differ from your plans. (For example higher or lower sales figures, more or less demand from customers)

- Where and when your product or service can be sold.

- How to set realistic sales targets.

SELF-SKILLS AND AWARENESS CHECKLIST

Yourself, your skills and your abilities	No idea 1	2	3	Could answer confidently 4
● How to work out how much money you need to live on, taking into account any tax credit and/or benefits.				
● What gross income your business needs to make to give you the money you need to live on				
● Different ways that your skills, abilities and knowledge can be developed.				
● How to diary and plan work. (e.g. by setting short and long-term targets, breaking down targets into smaller activities in terms of importance and urgency and estimating the time involved).				
● How you can save time. (For example efficient use of meetings and communications, minimising interruptions, delegating tasks to others.)				
● What information can be used for making decisions about managing time? (For example what you know and understand and what other people suggest.)				
● What things can be used to show improvements? (For example things that can be measure like customer satisfaction or better relationships.)				
● What gives you a sense of achievement? (For example meeting a deadline, finishing a piece of work, closing a sale, and getting praise from a customer.)				
● Your strengths and weaknesses in managing time.				
● What gets in the way of your work? (For example interruptions, stress, worry and tiredness,)				

Yourself, your skills and your abilities	No idea 1	2	3	Could answer confidently 4
• What (other than money) you can put into your business. (For example time, commitment, enthusiasm and creativity).				
• What you hope to get from running your business. (For example financial rewards, personal achievement, independence, business success).				
• The benefits and disadvantages of running your own business.				
• What you need to put into your business to make it work and how this may affect your current lifestyle.				
• How to analyse your aims in the short term (one year), medium term (two to three years) and long term (four years or more).				
• The difference between your own personal needs and the needs and aims of your business.				
• How to identify risks and how much risk you feel comfortable taking.				
• What technical skills & experience you have in making the product or providing the service that your business will sell.				
• What operational skills you have which will make your business work. (For example bookkeeping, getting supplies of raw materials, maintaining equipment, monitoring quality, and providing administrative support).				
• What managerial skills you have. (For example leading people, marketing research, new ideas and creativity.)				

Yourself, your skills and your abilities	No idea 1	2	3	Could answer confidently 4
• What you need to be able to do in the short, medium and long term to run your business successfully. (For example paperwork, sales, marketing, finance, production, purchasing, business law, getting supplies, maintaining equipment, monitoring quality, getting publicity, writing promotional materials, strategic thinking, communication, dealing with stakeholders, leadership, negotiation, decision-making, problem-solving, delegation etc.)				
• Your ability to deal with opportunities and threats. (For example, any changes in the market, new technologies, and threats from competitors or meeting new laws & regulations).				
• How you could improve your contribution to business success (for example, delegating work to others, recruiting more staff, training yourself and others.)				
• How to judge your own performance.				
• How to decide which skills and knowledge you need to develop and who might be able to help you decide.				
• What might make it difficult for to develop your skills and knowledge.				
• What different ways there are to develop your skills and knowledge and where to find out about them. (E.g. books, the internet, business advice, business mentoring, other businesses and contracts, workshops, conferences, training programmes and courses.)				
• How to work out the benefits and costs of developing your skills and knowledge. (For example, the fees, loss of time, extra wages for substitute staff.)				

Yourself, your skills and your abilities	No idea			Could answer confidently
	1	**2**	**3**	**4**
• Why it is important to be effective and efficient.				
• How to compare what you want to do with what you actually do. (E.g. use a diary or a work log to note that you plan, then compare with what you did, review your time a few days each month and note your progress.)				